# THE RENAISSANCE AND REFORMATION

The

# RENAISSANCE
and
# REFORMATION

A Short History

JOHN F. H. NEW

*John Wiley & Sons, Inc.*

NEW YORK · LONDON · SYDNEY · TORONTO

Library of Congress Catalog Card Number: 69-19928
Cloth: SBN 471 63340 2     Paper: SBN 471 63341 X
Printed in the United States of America

# Preface

This brief book is intended for general readers as well as for students who have little or no acquaintance with the period. It offers a narrative with occasional hints of the more difficult problems facing historians, and its brevity allows the student ample time for collateral reading in the sources and in the more advanced and interpretive secondary literature. The volume is part of a projected short history of Western civilization that is being prepared in collaboration with Professors C. Warren Hollister, William B. Slottman, and John L. Stipp. Two sections of this work, by C. Warren Hollister, have been published under the titles, *Roots of the Western Tradition: A Short History of the Ancient World* and *Medieval Europe: A Short History* (Second Edition). Very soon the entire work will be published, both as a series of paperbacks and in a cloth-bound format.

During the writing I enjoyed the help and the patience of C. Warren Hollister and William L. Gum. I am also grateful to Nancy Lipscomb, who gathered the pictures, and to Michael Craton for valuable suggestions.

JOHN F. H. NEW

*Great Eversden,*
*Cambridge, 1969*

# Contents

# List of Maps

MAPS BY JOHN V. MORRIS

# THE RENAISSANCE AND REFORMATION

# 1

# The Late Middle Ages

Change, decay, renewal, and reformation are the themes of this study. These are the perennial themes of history, but the changes that occurred between the 14th and 17th centuries were so large, so significant, and so swift that the period has been viewed with the heady excitement or the horrified fascination of most European historians.

The 13th century was the last century of relative peace that Europe was ever to enjoy. Of course there were wars, but they were local in character. Wars did not sweep continents and embroil multitudes of nations. It was a century of what we would now call contained conflicts: civil wars in Italy and England; steady extensions of monarchical power over great fiefs in France; and, after the revival of monarchy in England, following a series of limitations placed on the Crown by the barony, English attempts to conquer Wales, Ireland, and Scotland. The extent and scope of these wars were limited: the dreams of pan-European conquest and hegemony, which both earlier and modern times witnessed, had not yet been revived.

The 13th century was also a high point in the power of the Papacy. Outwardly Christendom was unified in religion, a uniformity that was to pass from history forever. Powerful heresies did, in fact, rankle and spread beneath the surface of Papal power: Innocent III launched a Crusade (1209) to destroy the Waldensians and Cathari (Albigensians) who were concentrated

1

particularly in Southern France. Their lives were pure but their thought was dualistic, resurrecting the Manichean view of the separate nature of the powers of good and evil against which St. Augustine had struggled in the 5th century. Outwardly the power of the Papacy was vindicated, and the heresies crept underground. And the relative peace of Europe resulted, in part, from the ability of the Papacy to channel the aggressive drives of feudal Europe outward against the heathen. The spirit of Christendom was still supremely confident and expansive.

A semblance of peace, the sway of the papacy, and the attack on the heathen presupposed and also created a community in Europe that has never arisen since, except in ephemeral ways. The growth of universities—tiny communities of scholars, as they were at first—is evidence of a pervasive culture accepted everywhere. There was one common language for the literate— medieval Latin—and university curriculums did not differ much from place to place.

Unity was the ideal for which the best minds strived: unity of the soul with God; unity of new thought into a systematic Christian philosophy; and unity of the faithful against the Moslem Saracens. This unity and community were preserved by a highly structured society. Each man—king, noble, knight, burgher, freeman, peasant, and serf—had his obligations, his duties, his rights, and his place. Position in society depended on service and office rather than on land ownership or wealth, although wealth and land were often the reward of service. These services and the duties of office were clearly delineated and well understood. The peasant owed so much labor for the use of his land, the knight owed so many days of military service on certain occasions, the noble owed so many taxes and so much support on fixed occasions, and his job was to advise the king and consent to his governance. The king was to administer justice and to protect the people. Whenever the proper duties were not performed, reprisals followed. Duties were known, customs were hallowed, the way to salvation was clear and assured, and one's place in society was secure.

All this emphasizes an order and orderliness that existed more in theory than in practice. There was a great gap between everyday reality and aspiration. Europe was still full of woods, wolves, and wild boar. The landscape was disorderly, and so was everyday life. Villeins and laborers were at the mercy of their overlords who might be cruel and extortionate. Distances seemed greater then than now; journeys were arduous. Communication was slow; mobility was local (indeed, peasants were not meant to leave the manor); and armies rarely moved 20 miles a day. A man from a neighboring village would be a conspicuous stranger; travelers were to be wondered at. Because horizons were so near, credulity was rank. Life for the many poor was "nasty, brutish, and short."

Change was an insidious fact of life. An ever-increasing use was being made of money as a substitute for feudal military obligations. Trade in Europe had been increasing steadily for several centuries, and the 13th century was a period of unparalleled prosperity for those who shared the surplus. It was a society that had discovered a sublime new style of architecture and had money enough and men skilled enough to build the monumental Gothic cathedrals that stand to this day.

In the realm of the mind, St. Thomas' theology was the counterpart to the Gothic cathedral: a vast, sometimes rambling, yet symmetrical system of thought carrying human reason to the very threshold of heaven. Here was novelty, but it was judicious novelty, a synthesis. Also the growth in wealth and numbers of artisans and burghers was an unstartling, gradual growth. Above all, the rise and spread of new religious orders symbolize the buoyant activity and optimistic faith of the century. A monk's life, like a peasant's, was geared to regularity. This ideal may have compensated somewhat for the capricious and precarious nature of existence.

Contained wars, prosperity for the higher classes, community, outward unity of faith, papal predominance, an ideal of order, social stability—all this was to pass in the next century. The exhilaration of the 13th century paled and faded, and the thick foilage of faith and reverence began to grow thin. The economic and territorial expansion of Europe ceased; the impressive certainties of scholasticism dissolved; and the unity of the Church and the political hegemony of the papacy were broken, never to revive. The relative stability of the social structure gave way to sudden flux and increased mobility; the sense of community was challenged by powerful divisive forces. A great civilization was dying and another was struggling to be born.

## THE CLOSING OF THE FRONTIER

The old balance of power in Europe was being violently transformed in the 14th century. For six centuries, the civilizations of Latin Christendom, the Byzantine Empire, and Islam had vied with one another without disrupting their rough equilibrium. Of the three, Latin Christendom had proved the most aggressive and successful, driving the Moors from Spain, the Turks from the Holy Land, and carving territory from the Slavic peoples in Northeastern Europe. But Latin expansion at the expense of Byzantium opened the way, by weakening the Empire, for a reinvigorated Turkish thrust into Europe. In 1354 these Mohammedans gained a foothold on the Continent and, before the turn of the century, had extended their dominion over the Balkans and were in a good position to control the mouth of the Danube. Thus, the large section of Christian territory south of the Danube from the Black Sea to the Adriatic was cut off from the West, and the fall of Constantinople (1453) was merely a matter of time.

Concurrently, the Teutonic Order (of German knights and princes), which had been driving from the Balkan coast toward the Black Sea, was thwarted by the unification of Lithuania and Poland as one Christian kingdom. Jagiello, King of the Lithuanians, prudently married the heiress to the Crown of Poland in 1386 and his conversion to Christianity negated the Order's *raison d'être:* the claim that they were carrying on a holy crusade. Under Jagiello, Poland-Lithuania joined Europe; but further expansion against the ferocious Muscovites and Tartars to the East was impossible. Europe had reached the end of its tether, and no new frontiers were to beckon and inspire for another century.

As important as the external frontiers were the internal frontiers of uncultivated land: the forests and fens, and moors and marshes that had been steadily reclaimed for profit and to ease the pressure of population. One cannot give a precise date for the dwindling in this supply of virgin land, but the saturation point was probably reached during the first half of the 14th century, although naturally the variations from place to place were wide. Some areas cultivated more land before 1350 than they cultivated again until the 18th century, and we know that

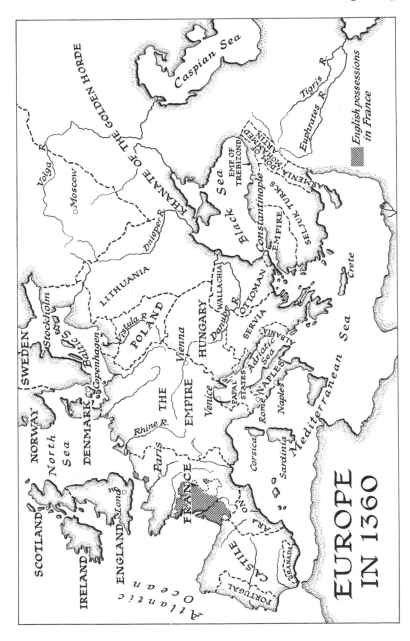

EUROPE
IN 1360

other areas in northern France and England sustained more people than they were able to sustain again until the 19th or even the 20th centuries. As the opportunities for agricultural exploitation were drying up, the thirst for self-realization had to be slaked by other pursuits. Thus, if, on the one hand, the closing of the frontiers implied hardship and frustration, on the other, it hastened the processes of social and entrepreneurial change.


RETRENCHMENT

The shifts and disruptions in the balance of power were accompanied by a relatively sudden and sharp economic relapse. War and pestilence (those inveterate enemies of trade) brought on a profound depression in the 1300's that lasted well into the 15th century. Allowing for fluctuations, the real prices of all the main lines of medieval produce dropped drastically: at the end of the 1400's, wheat in England brought less than half the silver it had brought at the beginning of the 1400's. In Prussia, rye prices (in silver) shrank by half over the 15th century. Customs accounts tell us that England's wool trade waned over these two centuries, and the Italian centers (particularly Florence), which were dependent on English raw material, suffered accordingly. Another stand-by of medieval commerce—the wine trade—was hard hit by recurrent crises. Exports of tuns or barrels from Bordeaux fell from a flood to a trickle; and, similarly, the salted herring trade, a good index of the salt industry, suffered constriction.

Mining industries entered various phases of exhaustion; Cornish tin production all but stopped, and the rich silver mines of Central and Southern Europe regressed. Apart from the damage wrought by external causes, output declined because seams petered out or because the digging of deeper seams raised problems of ventilation and water seepage that technology could not immediately overcome. In the second half of the 15th century, a revival occurred when improved drainage machines and better methods of ventilation made it possible to mine at greater depths than before in shafts 150 to 600 feet deep.

The falling off in new supplies of precious metal encouraged governments to debase their coinage (that is, to reduce the amount of precious metal in the currency) so that two contrary trends seemed to be at work: falling returns of bullion and rising "current prices," or inflation. In terms of purchasing power, a fortune of 22,000 French francs in 1200 was worth 16,000 francs in 1300; 7500 francs in 1400; 6500 in 1500; and, after the influx of Spanish-American silver in the 16th century, the 6500 francs fell to 2000 francs. Inflation never ceased, but at first it was related to debasement and only later to the cheapening of bullion through oversupply.

These conditions benefited the producer rather than the *rentier*; and although large individual fortunes continued to be made, savings were more easily lost. The countryside declined relative to the town, and in the cities the distance between merchants and artisans broadened into a gulf—a rift that resulted from the decline of artisans rather than from the rise of merchants. Class warfare became endemic. The craft guilds, facing shrinking markets and diminishing returns, tightened their restrictions on workmanship and membership. Since fewer members now had the chance to become masters, journeymen's guilds sprang up across Europe, expressing artisan resentment and representing demands for higher wages. In spite of their best efforts, the guilds were losing their grip.

Rapidly diminishing returns had a more pressing effect on vast landholders like the Church. With its land rents receding and other incomes crippled by inflation, the Church was forced to step up its campaign for revenue at the very time when tithes and other annates were becoming more burdensome to pay.

Equally, kings, finding themselves unable to live off their own private revenues, resorted to currency manipulation and to new forms of taxation to support their administrations. The period is one of growing governmental concern with trade (customs revenue) and with social conditions (internal security). Late medieval state promotion of business anticipates an age of mercantilism yet to come.

This general discussion paints an overall picture of recession, but it would be wrong to imagine that the depression was without touches of relief. As village fairs or village markets declined, towns flourished. Successful capitalists began to direct their far-flung enterprises from fixed headquarters. Hard times prodded businessmen into streamlining their operations; for instance, double-entry bookkeeping, the basic form of modern accounting, came into use in northern Italy early in the 14th century. The famous treatise of Pacioli the Florentine, which appeared in 1494, was merely the clearest exposition of an already common practice. Early in the 14th century also, the Venetian government built and continued to maintain a large fleet of ships specifically for trade with England and Flanders. The fleet, known as the Flanders Galleys, was hired to the highest bidders each year to gather wool and wool cloth, tin, cattle, and skins in return for dyed silks, spices, pearls, cotton, and Venetian glass. Their regular voyages lasted until 1532. Depression, then, forced upon commerce both rationalization and centralization, which are characteristics of modern capitalism.

If capitalism was purified in the fire of depression, there were striking variations within particular localities and decisive shifts in predominance from state to state. The success story of the era was the improvement in English woolen cloth manufacture and the boom of this English trade at the expense of the Flemish. The English never lost this supremacy. Florence, meanwhile, improved her cloth making with better dyeing and cloth finishing and, after setbacks through warfare in the late 14th century, her fine stuffs emerged unrivaled. In the 15th century the basic shift in Florence was from wool to silk cloth. Florence also captured the banking supremacy of Europe from Bruges in Flanders, mainly by winning the account of the papacy. But the Medici family of Florence in turn lost imperial custom to the German family of Fugger, who made an unbelievable fortune from mining and banking and lost it before the end of the 16th century by honoring the credit of bankrupt Spanish rulers. As Bruges declined after 1400, Antwerp rose by offering complete freedom from restrictive regulations and, after the discovery of America, Antwerp became the commercial capital of Europe.

Thus the late 14th century could boast of ups as well as downs —the English cloth trade is an example. Some industries recovered in the late 15th century, others did not; some cities, like Bruges, lost their commercial preeminence suddenly, whereas others, like Venice, receded imperceptibly over centuries. Neither the depression nor the partial recovery was uniform but, despite irregularities, the contraction of the 14th century was a continent-wide phenomenon and demands a continent-wide explanation.

## THE DECLINE OF POPULATION AND THE PLAGUE

It seems clear that Europe's population had been stagnant for two decades before the plague struck. Whether this resulted primarily from a contraction in opportunities, a response to shorter supplies of gold and silver, or inevitably from a growing disproportion of the sexes, we do not know. In any event, the plague confirmed a tendency already under way. But the plague itself can be considered as part of the cycle of subsistence agriculture, inevitable soil depletion, crop failure and periodic famine, and susceptibility to disease. That cycle had always been there, this particular plague was new. It was bubonic plague that arrived by the trade routes to the east, possibly through Alexandria or Baghdad. It seems to have spread northeast from India. One chronicler thought the plague entered Europe by way of Italian merchants caught in the Tartar Seige of Caffa, north of Constantinople. The Tartars were stricken with the disease as they besieged the city, but they turned sickness to a military advantage by projecting infected bodies over the walls. A ship from Caffa carried the merchants and the infection to Genoa (1347); from that time, it spread and flourished throughout Europe (1348-1350). Black rats carried the virus; fleas and contact with other infected persons transmitted it. Chroniclers placed the mortality figures exceedingly high: in Siena, four out of five died; at Avignon only a quarter of the population survived; and, at Pisa, 70 of every 100 died.

> In thirteen hundred and forty-eight
> Of one hundred there lived but eight.
> In thirteen hundred and forty-nine
> Of one hundred there lived but nine.

Here, no doubt, requirements of rhyme dictated this sense. Historians have taken contemporary reckonings with a grain of salt. Data from monastic records in England suggest that in the first attack the plague killed about one third of the population—more in the cities than in the country, more lowly than rich.

Europeans were entirely susceptible, but successive epidemics throughout subsequent decades were not as severe because many people were then immune. The plague recurred in the 15th century, again in the 17th and 18th centuries, and extremely isolated cases occur to this day.

An acute manpower shortage followed the decimation with predictable effects on particular occupations. Gradually many landowners turned from arable culture to grazing, since less help was needed. With labor still in high demand, the serf was able to bargain his way to freedom, especially in the West. The movement of the serfs to freedom had been occurring long before the plague, but the trend was reinforced by pandemic disasters. Landlords and governments tried to keep workers in their place and to hold down wages, but to little avail. The liberation of serfs was one of the inexorable social developments of the late Middle Ages. Rising wages also may have improved the lot of laborers. So the Death rewarded many in this world whom it could not carry off to the next.

In the Church, countless parishes lost their clergymen just when the populace was clamoring for sacraments, especially for absolution and the last rites. There occurred a spiritual denudation and impoverishment that was to last for centuries. Parishes were filled with the nearest available clergy, irrespective of education, so incompetence made its way in the wake of the plague. Complaints about "dumb dogs" in the pulpits were one response to the lowering of standards.

Although the estimate of 1 death out of 3 (or, more conservatively, 1 out of 4) is considerably lower than contemporary estimates, it illustrates graphically that hardly anyone would have been unaffected by the swift and horrible passage of the disease, with its swellings, inflammations, chest pains, vomiting, and blood spitting. In human terms the exaggerations of chroniclers are accurate measures of a holocaust of death. No modern war has been so destructive; corpses have never been so ubiquitous.

The moral and mental shake-up caused by the successive visitations of pestilence put a gruesome seal on the Middle Ages. Some people, who interpreted the plague as a wrathful punishment from God, went into paroxysms of piety. Others, realizing that death was imminent and inescapable, indulged in feverish debauchery and extravagance; still others practiced moderation and shunned society like the storytellers in Boccaccio's *Decameron*. In the long run, hedonism and ribaldry made most headway, but many people embarked on quests for new religious values; and, for a time, there was an upsurge of bizarre and macabre taste, and an outbreak of hysterical behavior. Groups of people, called Flagellants, formed into bands that traveled from town to town where they flayed each other with whips and chains in penance for the sins of the world. Dancing manias (known as St. John's or St. Vitus' dance) seized whole villages and townships. Men, women, and children, losing all control, danced until they could dance no more, shrieking and seeing visions. Anguish and ecstasy were the visible signs of inner torment. Terror and despair had caused mass hysteria and, although these aberrations were usually the outlets of the poor and simple folk and were banned by the Church, they remind us that the traumas of the 14th century wrought revolutions in men's minds as much as in the physical conditions of daily life.

### THE DISINTEGRATION OF SCHOLASTICISM: NOMINALISM

It is a mistake to suppose that the imposing synthesis of St. Thomas Aquinas swept the field in his own day. Conservative contemporaries criticized him sharply and, ironically, it was only as radical onslaughts on him gathered momentum that his views became hallowed orthodoxy. Conservatives had been shocked by Thomas' method of proceeding from the tangible evidences of creation to the nature of God, from effect to cause, rather than from cause to effect. St. Thomas distinguished reason from revelation, but used reason to complement revelation (as if revelation needed support). Moreover, having distinguished the two, he unified them by making all reason identical to God's, and by treating most truths as rationally verifiable (which, to a conservative eye, seemed to detract from the dignity of revelation). From an earlier vantage, St. Thomas was a revolutionary: the first radical "natural" theologian. That is, he grounded his theology on alleged uniformities of nature and constructed it by sheer intellection. But he was also a profound conservative, since he preserved the essentials of the Christian faith against the threat of new evidence and Aristotelian ideas by absorbing the new into the old.

The radicals used rigorous logic and sense experience as the touchstones of truth, and they did not agree with the rationality of Thomas' views.

John Duns (1265-1308)—a Franciscan of Scottish birth; hence called Duns Scotus—was a penetrating critic rather than a constructive scholar. His dialectical brilliance won him the nickname "The Subtle Doctor." But his fine distinctions and endless logic-chopping were extremely tedious. His name became a byword for the worst in scholasticism, for fruitless complications and, by some sardonic trick of history, for an ignorant and simple-minded person or dunce.

Since Duns believed that immortality could not be proved, he was critical of St. Thomas' arguments on this point. Similarly, he questioned Thomas' most celebrated proof of the existence of God—that the evidences of motion presupposed an unmoved mover—by rejecting the deduction as unproved. In logic, Thomas' presupposition involves what is known as the *a posteriori* fallacy or the "there's something behind it" argument, and a very useful "fallacy" it is. Duns used *a posteriori* argument in his own proof of the existence of God. Other differences between Duns and Thomas are variations in emphasis. Essentially both men were natural theologians with a large respect and sensitivity for philosophy. But Duns' probing criticisms, even though well intended, reduced Thomas' authority before it had become established.

A direct challenge to Thomism came from a devout English Franciscan, William of Ockham. He was never Duns' disciple. Indeed, he was only a boy when Scotus died, but Duns was often his point of departure. Ockham blended earlier elements of thought into a coherent philosophy of nominalism. In Latin, *nomen* means name. Nominalists believed that in discussing things they were really discussing the names of things and not the realities. "Realists" rejected this view. The difference between the schools of thought was most plain whenever they considered generic terms, or universals, like "mankind." Is the term a mere name symbolizing qualities common to many individual things? Or does it portray a reality over and above a sum of individual attributes? Thomas and Duns had been moderate realists; that is, they believed that universals had a reality of their own, although these universals were contained within their individual exemplars and were not separate entities. Ockham argued that universals had no reality and no existence whatsoever, except as mental concepts. To substantiate this view, he had three choices: (1) to deny some fundamentals of doctrine as they were then understood, (2) to consciously recast metaphysics, or (3) to abandon the effort to confirm doctrine by reason. Ockham chose the third course: revelations had to be accepted as miraculous. Not even the existence of God could be demonstrated. Thus, natural theology not only was occasionally fallacious—it was impossible. In this fashion, Thomas' happy marriage of reason and revelation was annulled in the 14th century.

Later nominalists considered reason and faith as being so incompatible that they revived the doctrine of double truth, which concluded that what was true in nature was not necessarily true in theology and that reason was neither divine nor capable of making Christian metaphysics intelligible. Even though revelation could violate the ordinary principles of morality and common sense, it was the higher truth. This notion of two kinds of truth was not an evasive sophism. Instead, it set religion above and beyond mortal understanding. Consequently, where nominalism prevailed, philosophy became unhinged from religion, and although philosophy lost standing it won more freedom of action. Revelation gained in status and in mystery. While Ockham gave complete obedience to the faith of the Catholic Church, there would be others who would seek their revelation in the scriptures or in the recesses of their own spirits.

### MYSTICISM

Mysticism is as old as religion, and has always been a main current in Christianity. Basically its motive force is a passionate desire to be united with the deity—a selfish desire that can become transmuted into a pure and selfless urge. Whether mysticism took an active, passive, pensive, or mindless form depended on how the mystic hoped to achieve the beatific union. Intellectually, at least, mysticism was a lonely business. But it renewed the spirituality of the Church and it also spawned ideas that the Church could not condone. It was, of course, a recurring spiritual phenomenon. In this instance, it grew out of the social and intellectual dislocations of the 13th century, and gained popularity during the greater disruptions of the 16th century.

A German Dominican called Master Eckhart (1260-1327) accepted the theology and philosophy of St. Thomas Aquinas, (Thomism) but gave it a luminous gloss that completely changed its appearance. Unlike St. Thomas, Eckhart believed that the Creator (at least, in His outward aspect) could be known in this life. Indeed, every person was part of His being, and only needed to retire into the "citadel of the soul" to realize it. God was everything, and nothing had existence outside Him. This may seem to be thoroughgoing natural theology, but it was not. Thomas had used the creation to clarify higher revelation; for Eckhart, the world was the revelation; and blessedness consisted in knowing that the fusion of oneself and all things in the oneness of God was an accomplished fact. Yet, ultimately, the Godhead, the pure "I am who I am" hidden within the creation, was unknowable, beyond definition and above human thought. Eckhart exhorted believers to concentrate on their union with this mysterious Deity, and also emphasized the need for Christ-like service. Knowledge of the truth would stimulate and sustain Christian action. Eckhart's mysticism was both contemplative and active. His successors retained these two qualities, although none was as daring a speculator as Eckhart. Although his writings were condemned for their pantheistic tendencies two years after his death, his influence filtered into various devotional movements: in particular, to the Brethren of the Common Life who later educated Erasmus. Some of Eckhart's ideas were reflected in an anonymous 15th century work, the *Theologia Germanica* (which Luther loved), and in St. Thomas à Kempis' *Imitation of Christ* (which everybody loved).

Fourteenth- and 15th-century mysticism returned to early neo-Platonic theology for inspiration just as many humanists and artists were finding refreshment in Platonic and neo-Platonic classics. The trend in humanism ran parallel to this religious platonism. Mystical theology was relatively unconcerned with the sacraments and the mediation of the Church, since one's direct relationship with God was all important. This kind of thinking may have helped Protestantism along, but Eckhart was not a Protestant pre-Reformer; he was a Catholic reformer who contributed much toward the Catholic Reformation in the 16th century by sowing devotionalism and piety in a church growing arid with intellectualism.

In different ways, nominalism and mysticism severed the Thomist synthesis. Nominalism attacked its rationality, and mysticism attacked its spirituality. Thomism survived, but scholasticism no longer possessed unifying principles. The schools warred with each other, and their failing power to pursuade foreshadowed the disintegration of the universal Church.

### HERESY

Looking back from the 17th century, the Puritan John Milton mourned that English prelates had perversely suppressed John Wycliffe's teachings. If they had not, he thought, the names of Hus, Luther, and Calvin would never have been known, and all the glory of the Reformation would have been England's. But again, as with mysticism, heresy was not one nation's prerogative. During every advance of the Turks, heresy spurted in Europe. Far from holding firm in the face of the challenge, the Church entered a period of schism and disunity when the situation demanded maximum unity and effort.

John Wycliffe (about 1328-1384) was truly a Protestant pre-reformer. But he arrived at his views by way of the old-fashioned philosophy of realism. Realism, for instance, led him to doubt the recently enunciated doctrine of transubstantiation (the idea that bread and wine change in some essential yet intangible way into the actual Body and Blood of Christ) in the Eucharist. However, Wycliffe's theology, like that of St. Thomas, was really an attempt at a synthesis of reason and revelation by the use of scripture, logic and Augustinian insights. He was the last of the great scholastics; and his originality is evidence of the provocative influence of St. Thomas in the history of thought.

In 1372 Wycliffe attacked the papal dominion, arguing in favor of lay confiscation of ecclesiastical property. And, for a time, he became the intellectual champion of the anticlerical faction in the state, offering this faction theological grounds for opposing the export of bullion to Rome. He enunciated the revolutionary doctrine that power and ownership should only belong to those who were ethically upright; that is, to those who showed palpable signs of grace in good behavior. The fact that he was intensely career minded and therefore bitterly frustrated when he did not receive the preferments he thought his talents merited may explain this period of his career but not the next.

During 1378 he underwent a spiritual deepening; he became a theologian instead of a political propagandist. Pamphlets, tracts, and sermons, in both Latin and vernacular English, poured from his pen. Because this work was written for the moment, it was not well organized but it was prolific. He sponsored the literal translation of St. Jerome's *Vulgate* into English, then began revising the stilted English translation into free-running prose. His secretary completed this work after his death. The Lollard Bible was visible evidence of his belief in the scriptures rather than traditions as the source of truth. The word Lollard meant either a wandering singer or lazy fellow; and it was a term of abuse given to his followers because they wandered and ministered in plainest garb, relying on hospitality for their sustenance. The term Lollardy signifies the heterogeneous principles, beliefs, and practices of the Lollards.

Wycliffe emphasized the doctrine of predestination and the fact that the true Church was composed only of chosen persons. He further stressed that only God's grace permitted election, a nascent version of Luther's doctrine of justification by faith alone. Logically it followed that the veneration of saints and relics was unnecessary, as was also the episcopal organization of the Church.

His views on the Mass moved from the doctrine of transubstantiation to a belief that the true presence of Christ in the elements (which remained bread and wine) was a spiritual presence. Christ was "sacramentally," not corporeally, present in the host. Of the seven sacraments, he would have retained baptism, the Lord's Supper, marriage, and a modified form of ordination. He would have discarded Penance, Confirmation, and Extreme Unction. Above all, Wycliffe emphasized the need to return to the purity of the Apostles' time; and this became the chief character of later

Lollardy. At first an academic movement, it gained support from the gentry, then finished as an evangelical faith for poor people.

Although Wycliffe's ideas and emphases were to become fundamentals of Protestantism, his reformation failed. He had no printing press to carry his words to a larger audience, and his movement lacked powerful political support. Lollards were burned intermittently throughout the 15th century, but the movement never died.

Lollardy called on common folk to dedicate themselves to charity, meekness, and good behavior. Such an educated and widely traveled poet as Geoffrey Chaucer (1340-1400) recognized that it filled a profound spiritual vacuum. Unlike many of his pen portraits, the Lollard parson in *The Canterbury Tales* is not disparaged; on the contrary, the diligent, benign, poor, and holy pastor is idealized: he not only taught Christ's love and the ways of the Apostles but followed his own teaching, practicing what he preached.

Lollardy challenged the worldliness of the Church. Often, in the past, such movements of consecration had been welcomed and absorbed; as the Church's power and moral suasion waned, its intolerance and inflexibility waxed. Wycliffe died hearing the Mass, but in 1415 the Council of Constance ordered his bones exhumed and burnt. His ashes were cast into the river Swift, which flowed into the Avon, which joined the Severn to reach the narrow seas between England and Ireland and then the open ocean. From there, it was said, his ashes, like his doctrines, were dispersed around the world.

Czechoslovakian students at Oxford, not ocean currents, carried Wycliffe's Latin works to Bohemia where they became a partisan issue at the University of Prague. The split between orthodox and reform-minded students was complicated by long-standing national animosities between Germans and Czechs. For the most part, the Germans were nominalists and the Czechs were realists, like Wycliffe. Outright brawls between the two schools, including the professors, were not uncommon.

The leader of the realists was a former good-living, chess-loving student, John Hus (b. 1370), who had become serious about religion when he was ordained a priest (about 1400). He denounced the vice, corruption, and lack of discipline in the

Church. Winning support from high and low (mostly because he based his religious appeal on Czech nationalism), he preached in the Czechoslovakian language and introduced the singing of Czech hymns into the service. After a royal decree of 1409 had ousted the Germans from control of the University, Hus was elected Rector.

But this high post could not save him from excommunication. In 1414, he was summoned to the Council of Constance to answer charges of heresy. (This same Council ordered Wycliffe's bones exhumed.) Trusting a promise of safe conduct that was revoked after his arrival, he hoped to convert the Council to his views. It became apparent that he was far more conservative than Wycliffe: he did not doubt the miracle of transubstantiation, although he did agree that the true Church consisted of the elect, and was disposed to reduce the Pope's dominion. Furthermore, when pressed, he could find no good reason for denying the wine to laymen in the celebration of the Mass; and his declaration in favor of communion in both kinds (sub utraque specie) decided this vexed issue for his followers at home. The chalice, or cup, became the distinguishing mark of the moderate Hussites, called Utraquists. It was a foregone conclusion that Hus would be found guilty of heresy, and the fires that consumed him in 1415 inflamed both the national and religious passions of the Czechs.

Once loosed, the strings of orthodoxy released ideas more radical than those of Hus. In Southern Bohemia a group carried Biblical literalism to the extent of bringing in a Kingdom of Heaven on earth. They built a new Jerusalem, called Tabor, and handed down a patriarchal constitution to the people. The Czechs were the chosen people of God, successors to the Hebrews. The Taborites dispersed the orthodox clergy, confiscated ecclesiastical property, and despoiled the convents and monasteries. Even more extreme sects flourished in this chiliastic atmosphere. One, known as the Adamites, tried to recapture the halcyon days of Adam in Eden. They occupied an island, held all things in common, stripped themselves of their wealth and their clothes, and became so scandalous that a powerful moderate Hussite from nearby believed that they should be massacred.

Taborites and Utraquists united briefly to expel ill-manned crusades against them in 1420 and 1421. Then they fell out among themselves and involved all Bohemia in civil war. The nobility, having pocketed parcels of Church lands, fought for the Utraquists, who crushed the Taborites in battle in 1434. Exhausted for the moment, both the Church and the Bohemians were happy to accept a truce (1436) whereby communion in both kinds would prevail in practice, though not in theory.

Hussites survived, unrepentant and unpunished, into the 16th century, when they cast their lot with the Lutherans. Whereas Lollardy survived in England, but failed to capture the allegiance of the nation, the Hussites partly succeeded. Too often the Reformation of the 16th century seems to be a sudden and unprecedented event. In reality, its gestation was long and painful and its precursors were enabled to prepare the way by the steady decline of the papacy.

### THE DECLINE OF THE PAPACY: CAPTIVITY, SCHISM, AND CONCILIAR MOVEMENT

A self-imposed exile in France during most of the 14th century (1305-1378) did much to undermine respect for the pontiffs and sapped the moral authority of the supreme office of the Church.

Popes often had left Rome, but never for seven decades on end. The very length of the stay lost for the papacy much of its former influence, since Rome was the original and ancient seat of St. Peter's successors, the tomb of the Apostles, the resting-place of martyrs, and a city for pilgrimage. It had a symbolic significance that was part of the papacy itself and the Pope who had abandoned Rome was less of a Pope for doing so. Pious souls, even saints, begged the Popes to return, but they either could not or would not.

The reasons for their reluctance to return were perhaps more damaging to Christendom than the duration of their absence. As the nominee of the French king, it was understandable that Clement V (1305-1314) should be crowned in France. He need not, however, have decided to stay. Yet, stay he did at Avignon, and he pliantly suffered himself to be intimated and browbeaten by Philip IV, serving the royal will to the indignity of the papal office. Clement showed rank favoritism to the French clergy; of his first appointments, nine out of ten cardinals were

French. Thus the French contingent won control of the College with the result that all of the popes until the end of the absence were French.

The situation at Avignon appeared so ignominious that people referred to it as the "Babylonian Captivity," and one disgusted humanist called the papacy "Frenchified." From their position as international powers, the popes had succumbed to the prejudices of nationality. Their stay at Avignon loosened the close ties with Italy, weakened the affiliation with the Empire, and identified the papacy so intimately with one nation that Englishmen, Germans, and Italians could not feel as dutiful or as responsive to it as before.

Neither would the French: for previously the French Crown had to struggle to be free of papal interference; now, when the papacy was not being subservient, there was at least a mutual accommodation between the Church and the state. After the weak primacy of Clement V, neither king nor pope trespassed on each other's jurisdiction. In this respect, the captivity was a rehearsal of modern relationships between church and state.

Several of the Avignonese popes intended to return to Rome—but turmoil in the Papal States deterred them. The ruling family of Naples (to whom the government of the Papal States was delegated) failed to curb anarchy—the papal Vicars-General had no better success. Only when it seemed that the papal territory would be lost forever did Gregory XI (1370-1378) restore the Holy See to its home (1377).

Fear of trouble and preference for comfort seemed to have prolonged the popes' absence and their final return smacked of political desperation. From beginning to end, the Avignonese papacy had acted on principles of political expediency and, accordingly, its prestige was irreparably damaged.

Even the extensive administrative reforms of this period, undertaken by Clement's successor, John XXII (1316-1334), were to be geared to expediency rather than right. Like so many efficient administrators, John was spiritually shallow, if not obtuse. His only foray into theology was heretical and he was forced to recant before his death. He proceeded just as crassly against the evangelical wing of the Franciscan Order. Being of practical temper he thought people who refused to recognize the need for owning property must be deluded dreamers, so he declared them heretics and turned the Inquisition upon them.

His administrative reforms, though effective, bear witness to his spiritual destitution. The customary burdens on the clergy were increased, the maze of ecclesiastical courts was rigidly stratified, and the sale of church offices and benefices was systematized. In fact, by systematization, the sale of offices was legitimatized. Simony and venality came to stain the whole fabric of papal administration; thus, to honest Christians, the residence of the papacy at Avignon was not only a shame but a scandal.

No sooner had Gregory XI returned to Rome than his death caused a new election (1378) and thereby a greater disaster for the Church. Under pressure from an armed and clamorous crowd, and to the pealing of bells, the College elected an Italian who took the name of Urban VI. Promptly after the French cardinals had withdrawn from Rome they protested the election, claiming that their collaboration had been wrung from them by fear of the mob, and appointed a French Pope who called himself Clement VII. Who was to decide between the two popes? Prayers were offered on both sides; universities debated one way or the other. France and her friends (Scotland, Aragon, Castile, and Naples) acknowledged Clement, and this was enough to induce England, the Empire, Bohemia, Poland and, of course, Italy to cleave to Urban. In the last resort it was the good sense of statesmen and the selfish fears of the cardinals that all would come to ruin that prompted the calling of a General Council at Pisa in 1409. All, indeed, may have been ruined, since the first year of the schism was the year of the maturity of John Wycliffe's thought, soon to be followed by the Hussite movement in Bohemia. Despite the dangers, the two rival popes (Gregory XII of Rome and Benedict II) tried to sabotage the Council. But the Council deposed them both as schismatics and notorious heretics and elected Alexander V to the vacant office. Unfortunately Benedict and Gregory refused to be deposed, so now there were three.

Alexander's successor, John XXIII (1410-1415), called another council which opened at Constance in 1414. Doubtless, John hoped to emerge as the head of a united Church, but the Council turned against the man who called it and forced John to resign.

He thereupon tried to repair his loss by leaving the Council, an act that dissolved it according to canon law. The Council, however, stubbornly resolved not to disband and deposed John formally. It also induced Gregory to resign and, for the second time, branded Benedict as a heretic and a schismatic. Notwithstanding, he continued to consider himself the only true Pope until his lonely death in 1423. The Council—both cardinals and delegates —elected Martin V in 1417 and brought unity at last to the Western Church.

During the forty-year schism, the remaining shreds of veneration and respect were stripped from the papacy; Wycliffism (Lollardy) and Hussism flourished; and a revolutionary movement gathered momentum within the Church itself.

The conciliar movement was a revolution of necessity, occasioned by the schism. The Councils of Pisa and Constance had already set themselves above the popes and, having gained so much ground, cardinals and delegates were reluctant to lose it. Papal monarchy had actually become conciliar oligarchy.

Although obliged to call a Council, the new Pope, Martin V, was intransigently opposed to its spirit. When the Council of Pavia (1423) proposed church reform he promptly dissolved it. Similarly his successor, Eugenius IV, tried to dissolve the Council of Basel in 1432 when it argued reform. At that time the Council was powerful enough to force Eugenius to retract the bull of dissolution. But three years later Eugenius persuaded a minority of the Council (mostly Italians) to go to Ferrara to discuss an ecumenical union with the Greek Church. The majority at Basel continued to sit. In 1439 Eugenius transferred his Council from Ferrara to Florence and there won an overwhelming victory: a solemn pledge of union between the Roman and the Greek churches. It was a glorious triumph. After six centuries of disunity the broken Body of Christ was restored; East and West were joined together in one communion. The remnants of the Council of Basel were thoroughly discredited. Four years later the Eastern Church repudiated the ecumenical agreement; still, in the interim, the agreement had destroyed the pretensions of the Conciliarists.

Thus, by the middle of the 15th century, the papacy had outlasted captivity, schism, and conciliar revolution, but the toll was terrible. From top to bottom the Church remained unreformed; heresy had not been stamped out; the financial demands of the Curia had become more and more rapacious—particularly when rival popes were claiming the revenues—and the secular state had rid itself once and for all of effective papal interference.

This last political reality was supported by a growing body of political theory. Dante had set the secular authority above all other powers on the ground that peace was a prerequisite for humanity, and peace could be guaranteed best by the Emperor. Dante thus discarded St. Thomas' idea of two separate but equal and collaborating dominions; and Dante's emphasis was further developed by Marsilius of Padua (d. about 1340) and by the English nominalist William of Ockham. Ockham and Marsilius also had wanted the popes to be subject to Councils.

After Conciliarism failed, the practice of state sovereignty was never seriously threatened by the papacy again. France even managed to wring ecclesiastical independence from papal weakness. By the Pragmatic Sanction of Bourges—where the French clergy assembled in 1438—the sending of appeals and annates to Rome was forbidden; and the election of Bishops was taken out of the Pope's hands and given to the King and cathedral chapters. This declaration, issued as a royal ordinance, created an autonomous Gallican Church, which was as much as France wanted in the way of a Reformation. Papal ascendancy in politics was confined to the central Italian states, and eventually this limitation enforced a specialization in spiritual function on the Church. An essentially spiritual papacy was thus delivered from the temporal world in travail and in spite of itself.

In 1300 Boniface VIII had exclaimed with some justification, "I am Caesar—I am Pope!" By 1450, Eugenius IV was lucky to have a papacy to preside over. The mightiest institution of the Late Middle Ages had been brought low by internal disorders, by provincial political pressures, and by the pettiness of popes. During the process, for better or worse, one epoch of Christian history ended and another began.

# 2

# France and England:
# The Hundred Years War

The decline of the papacy prepared a way for those who built territorial rather than spiritual empires. The common effort against the heathen had passed; the happy synthesis of scholastic thought was under attack; and old certainties of faith were giving way. The expansive phase of medieval history had come to an end. Europe was hemmed in. The processes of overpopulation, overcultivation, and soil depletion were beginning to be felt before the terrible and recurring catastrophe of the Plague struck the Continent. Repeated crises aroused violent feelings.

Moreover, the long period of relative peace, over which the papacy had presided in the 13th century, had threatened to emasculate feudalism. Feudalism was based on the interlocking exchange of services (especially of military services) and, if the army fell into disuse, the hierarchy of power would seem less justifiable, less worthy of authority and prestige. Feudal society was geared for war. At first, then, the Hundred Years War can be called a revival of feudal spirit. But it can also be viewed as a form of feudal-monarchial loyalism that thrust itself into the vacuum left by the loss of a sense of community and unity in Europe. The war, fought sporadically over a period longer than a hundred years, actually resulted in the destruction of feudalism and in the rise of unified, national states. In the wake of war, serious social upheavals occurred. Peasant revolts broke out on both sides of the English Channel and, in France, there was a concerted attempt by the bourgeois to set the monarchy within constitutional limits. They failed, and would have to try again in another century when royal and feudal might was weaker. In England, after defeat, the nobility spent their last aggressive energies fighting a suicidal civil war; in France, after victory, the privileges of the nobility seemed vindicated, so they lived on. But, meanwhile, the French monarchy had strengthened its hold on the nation, and had developed a bureaucracy that depended on the Crown alone and from whose exercise of power the nobility of the sword were excluded. In France the Crown centralized its power against the nobility without their help, yet they lingered on; in England the Crown was able to centralize its power with the help of a largely new nobility, a loyal gentry, and bourgeois class. The net result was two centralized states and a new order from the chaos of Western Europe.

### THE CAUSES OF THE WAR

Ever since the Duke of Normandy had invaded England in 1066 the security of France had been more or less continuously in jeopardy, but recently the designs of England had been encouraged by the marriage of Edward II to Isabella, the 12-year-old daughter of Philip IV (the Fair) of France (1307). Along with youth, Isabella brought Edward a claim to the French throne. Philip's three sons, who were kings of France in swift succession, left no male heirs. Thus a question was raised to which there was no formal answer. If a female could transmit the regal inheritance (though not enjoy it herself), then Edward III's claim was valid, since Edward III was grandson through the daughter of Philip IV; but if succession could only be transmitted by the male line, then Philip of Valois, nephew of Philip the Fair, was the proper claimant. Precedent supported Valois (the daughter of Philip's first son had given up her claim in favor of his brothers), while Edward's alien status spoke against England. Philip was recognized as regent, then as King (the VI) which so mortified Edward that he determined at least to regain the Angevin lands lost over a century ago by King John, and if possible to win the Crown of

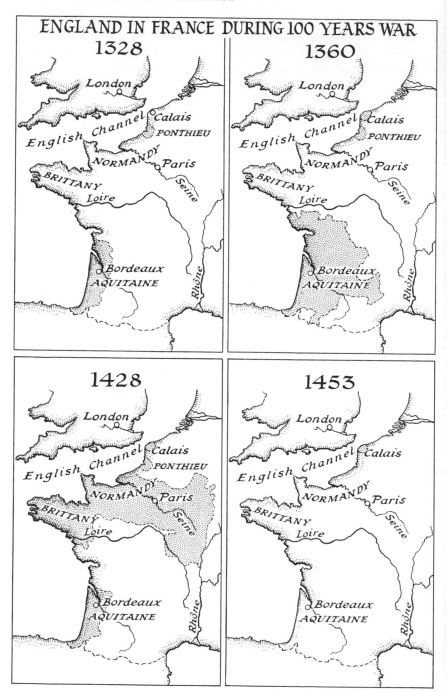

ENGLAND IN FRANCE DURING 100 YEARS WAR
1328
1360
1428
1453

France itself. In the first instance, then, it was a genealogical crisis that brought on the war.

But, of course, without the most powerful of royal lusts—desire of territory, hope of influence, and passion for prestige—there would have been no crisis. England's hold over what remained to her of Aquitaine—Guyenne—was being systematically undermined by every legal device and political trick imaginable, so that Edward either would have to fight or withdraw. It was finally the declaration by Philip that Guyenne was forfeitable that brought Edward across the Channel in 1337. Before this, Philip had flouted English interests by helping Edward's enemies in Scotland. And, by invading Gascony in 1333, he had thrown the substantial English trade in wine with the Continent, which was centered in Gascony, into serious disarray. There was also the matter of rivalry for the rich commerce of Flanders, although this rivalry seemed to be as much for the strategic value of an alliance as for reasons of trade. Indeed, at this time, England was emerging as the competitor of Flanders in wool clothmaking. But raw wool found a considerable market there and Edward reaped handsome revenue from its export. After harrassment at French hands, the Flemings had deposed their pro-French Count and had set up a clothier, one Jan Van Artevelde, as their ruler. Naturally he looked to England for protection and Edward III, with a heart full of chivalry and head full of shrewd calculations as well as dreams of grandeur, was eager to give it.

### THE WAR

Apart from lulls for plagues and truces and a peace between 1360 and 1369, the war falls into two main phases. One terminated when the minorities of Charles VI and Richard II came to an end (1388 and 1389, respectively). From that time a continuous series of truces lasted until 1406 when internal dissensions arose to preoccupy both parties. The second phase of the war did not begin until 1415 when Henry V invaded France afresh in headstrong pursuit of military glory.

England won the battles and France won the campaigns. Each phase of the war began with resounding English victories and ended with an effective retaliation and repulsion by the French.

English tactics were occasionally inspired, but they lacked an overall strategy. England's armies were really expeditionary forces. They were inadequate to occupy and to hold a large territory for a long period. The English operations reflect a freebooting rather than a conquering mentality (which indicates the development of their insular temperament), since England planned a series of ravaging campaigns with limited strategic objectives. This was a fair way to win glory and concessions but it was no way to conquer a country and capture a crown. The wonder of it is that England was able to carry its marauding so far—even to the gates of Paris. France was weakened by the division between the rival houses of Burgundy (whose emblem was a red scarf) and of Orléans (whose emblem was a white scarf); and the relative poverty of the French Crown gave an advantage to the English. English Parliaments were generous in support of war, mixing patriotism with their awareness that offers of subsidies made them more powerful in the counsels of the realm. At first, too, Edward had unlimited credit from a Florentine bank, which he used liberally to buy arms and token alliances before reneging on the debts and ruining his creditor.

All three of the great English victories were won when raiding expeditions met with concentrated forces. The Battle of Crécy (1346) derived its name from the plateau to which the English had retired in order to avoid a trap. They took up a strong position between a forest and a stream so that the French were forced to fight uphill on a narrow front. Edward placed his archers in the forefront. They broke the undisciplined charges of the French knights with a hail of arrows, and the knives of the foot soldiers finished the job. Arrows from a longbow of yew pierced defensive armor, and horses that were struck normally wheeled in terror and trampled those behind. A horseless, heavily armored knight was, of course, easy prey for the nimbler foot soldier. At Crécy the French were utterly routed, leaving a generation of chivalry dead on the field.

While the Battle of Crécy did not end the supremacy of cavalry in military history (for cavalry survived into the Second World War), it did usher in the age of the longbow. The French learned nothing from defeat, since they suffered again and again, at

Poitiers (1356) and Agincourt (1415). Each time, strong positions and the skill of the English archers more than compensated for overwhelming numbers against them.

After Crécy the English took Calais by seige and it remained in English hands for two centuries. But after Agincourt no major English victories were won on the Continent until the campaigns of the Duke of Marlborough three centuries later.

French victories were no less remarkable and were certainly less ephemeral. In the second phase of the war the tide was turned against England by a young peasant girl called Jeanne d'Arc (Joan of Arc) who heard voices in the woods, accompanied by visions of saints, urging her to rid France of the invader and have the Dauphin (son of Charles VI) crowned. She obeyed the call, went to the Dauphin to proclaim her mission and offered to relieve Orléans, which was then under seige and alone was keeping France from complete subjection to England. She met with doubt initially, but was given her chance. Clad in white armour, riding a white charger and carrying a white banner she entered Orléans and miraculously revived the city's spirit with her tranquil confidence. This so unnerved its attackers that they were driven off by the defenders in a few days. Then she begged the Dauphin to have himself crowned King of France (Charles VII) at Rheims. This was bold counsel indeed, for technically the infant son of Henry V was King of both England and France; and, practically, Rheims was in enemy hands. But Joan, mystically inspired, simply cut through both problems. The enemy dispersed at her approach and her presence consecrated the Dauphin's coronation. Joan then considered her mission accomplished and asked for permission to return home, but Charles found her inspiration useful and kept her at court where jealous factions sought her downfall. When she pressed for an immediate advance on Paris, she gained no support and her assault failed. Carrying on without full cooperation, she was soon captured by disaffected Burgundians who sold her to the English for 10,000 gold francs. The English prosecuted her in a tribunal of the Inquisition, dominated by a Norman bishop, claiming that she had bewitched the English soldiers. After a tortuous travesty of a trial she was found guilty of heresy and of sorcery. She was maltreated, condemned, and burned at the stake. She was not twenty. Although English soldiers mumbled at the time, "We have burned a saint," Joan was not canonized until 1920.

Charles VII, whom she served so well did not raise a finger to save her. He offered neither hostage nor a sufficient ransom. Yet his craven character should not blind us to the fact that he held (as did most medieval kings) a quasi-sacred position in the State. Without popular religious veneration for the institution of the monarchy, Joan could not have succeeded as far as she did.

It is often said that the gentle Maid of Orleans achieved more in death than in life. Martyrdom hallowed her inspiration; national resistance revived. The connection may not be so simple. Her contribution was to give "divine" legitimation to the Dauphin and, at a time when monarchs were the holders of sacrosanct office, her legitimation was important. But the Burgundians probably came over to Charles VII because they feared English ambitions against their own territory. And the death of Bedford had removed England's best commander. Town after town, province after province fell to the French. In the last encounter of the war at Bordeaux in 1453 the French employed a newfangled weapon called the cannon more effectively than before and cut the English troops to ribbons. Modern warfare had arrived.

All the victories, the diplomacy, the squandering of men and money, and the schemes of empire, so nearly achieved, went for nothing. Calais alone remained to the English. France was at last free to consolidate her geographical unity. England was to wage another hundred years war against France for colonies, but never again for continental territory. Thus her expulsion from France crystallized the outlines of Western Europe to the present day.


SOCIAL PROBLEMS


Long wars entail heavy expenditures as well as heavy casualties, and the necessary extortions of the French and English crowns brought social problems to light that otherwise might have remained dormant for centuries. Unlike England where the landowning classes bore the brunt of extraordinary government expenses, the burden of taxes in France fell upon the bourgeois and peasantry. It was inevitable, then, that the Estates General, incorporating the bourgeois in its third estate, should attempt to limit the royal prerogative in return for voting taxes. The Estates General wished to fix itself as a permanent power in the realm and demanded responsibility from the royal officials. Under the leadership of Étienne Marcel and supported by the bourgeoisie of Paris, the Estates General tried to establish constitutional monarchy in France (1357-1358). But their effort was undermined by a simultaneous social movement.

There was little in a bourgeois constitutional revolution to commend it to the peasant. Not only had he been oppressed by taxes but he had suffered the depredations of invaders who lived off the land and the murder, rapine, and pillage of local marauding bands. Although Paris and Marcel opposed the Dauphin, the peasantry vented their pent-up bitterness against the nobility. After all, the nobility had forsaken their function by failing to defend France against its attackers. An orgy of château-burning and molestation swept the countryside (1358). Indeed, for a time, these Jacqueries, as they were called ("Jacques" was a peasant garment), became organized. But their net effect was a double disaster: by association they discredited the reformist agitation of the Estates General and they united Dauphin and nobility in the desire of counterrevolution. Tens of thousands of peasants were massacred by the knights who had not been able to slaughter the English, and Marcel was assasinated with impunity.

Thus both the social and the constitutional revolutions failed: the interests of the bourgeois and the peasantry had proved harmful to one another. Paris' behavior underlined its importance in France, and from this time the city remained a dominant political influence until the defeat of the Commune of 1871.

Since England was not a theater of war, the position of its peasantry was quite different. Those who survived the plague, on the whole, had managed to improve their lot. Therefore, it was not depression and despair that unsettled them but a sudden threat to their new-found gains. In 1379 a graduated poll tax was devised to fill the war-drained coffers, and its novelty was that it fell upon everybody. Evasion was widespread until, in the spring of 1381, commissioners were dispatched to ensure full payment. This tightening up precipitated the revolt.

Peasants and artisans from the counties around London converged on the seat of government. One John Ball, a fiery priest, had imbued some of them with notions of social equality:

> When Adam delved and Eve span
> Who was then a gentleman?

so that their leader Wat Tyler had difficulty restraining them. Their demands were for freedom from villeinage and feudal service and for permission to lease their land instead.

With considerable courage, the young King Richard II faced the massed rebels outside London and promised concessions, hoping to disperse them. His promises were empty. Some of the rebels had already broken loose in the city and had begun to sack and slaughter. Wat Tyler, called to parley, was struck down by the Lord Mayor, and Londoners who were quickly galvanized into loyalty by fear of anarchy came out to help Richard disperse the rebels without further bloodshed.

One dispersal did not quell the discontent, and risings fanned outward from the counties around London. By summer, repression had set in and Parliament, full of landowners, solemnly denounced all concessions to tenants as base and illegal. Having failed to secure release from servitude and obligation by storm, the peasants over the next three centuries had to advance themselves as best they could. One thing was gained: the poll tax was never reimposed.

### INSTITUTIONAL DEVELOPMENTS

The fact that England did not see a concerted bid for power by Parliament tells something of the dissimilar institutional arrangements in the two countries. In France the Estates General of the nation as a whole were called infrequently and only for money; they were inexperienced; and they were divided into three distinct classes or "estates"—nobility, clergy, and commoners—with separate votes and meeting places. Unity was structurally unlikely. Also the Estates General of France shared or, more often, lost authority to the provincial Estates General, with whom monarchs had dealt individually. Delegates to the national meetings were circumscribed by the reluctance of the local bodies to give up their powers and influence. And kings found the local

Estates General more amenable to royal demands. Both lack of power and lack of servility hindered the development of the national body. The English Parliament had grown up around the barons who comprised the Great Council of the King, and whenever a broad base of support was sought, nobility, knights, and burgesses met to consider not only financial affairs but also legislative, and high judicial matters. From the time of the Magna Carta (1215) it was the barons who threatened the Crown and tried to control it, and they carried the lesser property owners along with them. Before the outbreak of the Hundred Years War, the lesser clergy had declined to sit in Parliaments, and the gentry had chosen to sit with the representatives from the boroughs rather than separately; so that in both the lower and upper houses of Parliament the landed interest predominated, and the two houses had a homogeneity unknown to the French Estates. A Statute of York (1327) had established that "great matters" were to be considered by the "community of the realm." Hence Parliament, in general, and Commons, in particular, had a security and a permanence in the affairs of state that the Estates General did not have. England needed no Étienne Marcel. Parliament, moreover, being the only body of its kind in the realm, was less hampered by the residual powers of local authorities.

The Commons of the English Parliament was not powerful—following the manner of its origin as an extension of the Great Council it remained subservient to the Crown and the magnates or, in the event of friction, to whoever was uppermost of Crown or magnates. This malleability ensured that Parliament (with the Commons) would continue. The story of the development of Commons' independence and self-consciousness belongs to the Tudor and Stuart age, but in the 14th century Commons did establish (in theory) its sole right to approve taxation and, though not its birth certificate, this right became a passport to continual life.

If Parliament was more deeply entrenched than the Estates General, France could boast of a more effective civil service than England. It had been inherited from the 13th century and had been extended to cope with the financial and administrative tasks arising with the war. Such a servile functionary class, and a courtier caste, did not develop to the same extent in England; and the fact that the French king could command administrators who were wholly dependent on the Crown gave him freedom of action that monarchs never enjoyed in England. Edward III had chosen a cheap way to promote government: he appointed leading gentry to the unpaid posts of Justices of the Peace (1361) and commissioned them to administer and adjudicate local matters. Apart from economy, this expedient had the advantage of binding local leaders to Crown policy; but, by the same token, it contained the disadvantage that royal policies depended on the good will of the gentry for their implementation.

Yet even in England (though more in France), personal monarchy was giving way to bureaucratic management. Inevitably the increase in national business called for an extension of existing household institutions to cope with it and, increasingly, the private functions in the royal household became public offices. Still the mystique of exalted and capricious medieval monarchy lingered on—it caused Joan of Arc to revere the supine Charles VII and English kings to imagine that they could cure scrofula with their touch—but a growing bureaucracy provided the continuity and stability that made it possible for monarchy to survive wars and tumults and to enter the vicissitudes of a new age unhumbled if not unscathed.

### FEUDAL FACTIONALISM

The principle of monarchy was never questioned, but throughout and after the Hundred Years War the place and the person of the Crown was often in doubt. A disputed succession, a child heir, or royal incompetence threw the highest prize of the state to the strongest bidder. This sort of instability was inherent in personal monarchy and it was the besetting defect of a militarily constituted society: if the Crown was weak or the nation was at war, the temptation, in a feudal context, for barons to build up private armies was irresistible; and all too frequently in the 15th century royal weakness and war emergency coincided. Through long usage, endemic warfare progressed from a vice to an addiction: the barons, knights, and nobles who cultivated ungentle arts in jousts and tourneys and applied them in battle became victims of their own warlike spirits.

Immaturity and periodic fits of insanity rendered Charles VI incapable of governing France (1380-1422); so the Dukes of Burgundy and Orléans vied with each other for power. Their struggles, murders, and massacres convulsed France in the period between the phases of the war and long after.

Phillip the Bold of Burgundy, being the uncle of both the King and Louis of Orléans, managed to hold supremacy until his death in 1404. Then the struggle devolved upon Louis and John the Fearless, Phillip's successor. When Louis was murdered in Paris in 1407 the Count of Armagnac stepped in to champion the Orléanist cause because his daughter had married Louis' son, Charles. Now the struggle became regional: Paris, northern France, and Flanders cleaved to Burgundy, while southern and central France supported Armagnac. Paris, as a focal point, was a scene of perpetual disorder, where mob was frequently king and the real king counted for nothing. Because of a bloody riot in 1413, John the Fearless lost control of the respectable elements in Paris and, without Paris, he was forced to capitulate to the Armagnacs. But his heart was not in it. When a traitor opened the gates of Paris to his followers in 1418 a brutal massacre of Armagnac supporters followed. Once again John was master of the city, but in the process of negotiations with the Armagnacs from a position of strength he was murdered, whereupon his successor, Phillip the Good, openly allied himself with the English for revenge. Yet alliances are fleeting; as the Orléanist (Armagnac) cause waxed and the English cause waned, and as the Protector of England was casting covetous glances at Burgundian lands in the Low Countries, Phillip came to terms with Charles VII (1435). From this time the success of France against England was assured. Still Burgundy was fickle; in the next generation Phillip's son, Charles the Bold, thought of consolidating a Burgundian state from the Low Countries to the Franche-Comté. This would have cut across Lorraine and Champagne, and would have threatened the independence of the Swiss cantons. At one stage Charles had Louis XI at his mercy, but released him only to be rewarded for his restraint with ruin, since Louis threw diplomatic and financial aid to the Swiss who, after a series of battles, finally killed Charles in 1477. This left only a daughter. Fearing Louis' attentions toward her territories, she married Maximilian of Hapsburg for protection and maybe love, thereby beginning a long tale of dynastic rivalry between France and the House of

Hapsburg. Louis XI, meanwhile, mopped up his other rivals at home by murder and beheadings. Not inappropriately he is known to history as the Spider King; yet his plottings laid the basis of French unification. In a labyrinth of alliances, of shifting loyalties, of turns and turnabouts, the importance of controlling Paris shines like a beacon to emphasize the importance of the urban centre in a struggle for power.

Blood, guile, and treachery attended these births of new nations. While Charles VI's weakness brought civil war to France, in England Richard II's minority encouraged coteries of barons to govern until he suddenly declared himself of age. Before he was thirty, he was overtaken by galloping megalomania and his irrational extortions so alienated the populace that when Henry of Lancaster came to claim his confiscated estates he found a kingdom for the asking. Accordingly he deposed Richard (1399) and assumed the crown by right of conquest and indirect inheritance, although Parliament also asserted itself in a subtle, obsequious fashion by electing him Henry IV (1399-1413).

This line of Lancasters destroyed itself at home by success in France. At the height of his conquests Henry V was recognized as regent of France (Treaty of Troyes, 1420) and his heir was recognized as the heir of two kingdoms. But by marrying Charles VI's daughter he formed the connection through which Charles' insanity could be passed on to his son. And this child was but 10 months old when he died (1422). To compound matters, Henry VI not only was a minor, subject to periods of insanity but, in his moments of lucidity, he was kind and gentle, meek and mild—quite unfit to rule at that time. The Duke of Bedford was named regent to defend his inheritance in France, and the Duke of Gloucester became Protector of England. A struggle for power developed between Gloucester and the Court party gathered around the French Queen, who was the opposite of her husband. She was sane, aggressive, and vicious. At Gloucester's downfall (and possibly murder) the opposition looked to Richard of York, son of the last son of Edward III. Two years after the Hundred Years War ended, the Queen's unwillingness to share power and her vindictiveness drove York to arms. Thus, with scarcely a break, civil war replaced foreign war.

York's emblem was a white rose and Lancaster's emblem was a

red rose. These Wars of the Roses saw the bloodiest fighting ever waged on English soil, yet the anarchy was neither universal nor unmitigated. Between 1455 and 1460 all of York's victories were followed by reversals, in the last of which he was killed. Then, at Towton in 1461, the forces of Edward, son of Richard, and of his too-powerful ally, the Earl of Warwick (called the Kingmaker), defeated the Lancastrians in a blinding snowstorm. York's line replaced Lancaster's.

Although Edward IV was a dissolute playboy (perhaps because he was a dissolute playboy), he was so popular that when the mighty Warwick turned against him he was able to destroy him, to confiscate his vast estates and to extinguish the direct Lancastrian line forever (1371). By encouraging trade, accepting a handsome "nonaggression" stipend from Louis XI of France, and making good use of confiscations and fines, Edward managed to avoid calling on Parliament for money. A pale light at best, Parliament went into eclipse. This eclipse and the rise of autocracy were the Yorkist's contributions to English constitutional development.

Worn out by not resisting temptation, Edward died leaving two sons. The eldest, at the age of 12, became Edward V for a short sad reign from the spring to the summer of 1483. He was at the mercy of his unscrupulous uncle Richard of Gloucester. By an unsubtle combination of bribery, slander, executions, and intimidation, Richard induced Parliament to declare him King, whereupon the princes were sent to the tower and were smothered in their sleep. Richard III knew no peace; he lived in danger of rebellion at home and in danger of attack from abroad. His worst fears were realized when Henry Tudor, a distant and indirect Lancastrian claimant to the throne, landed in Wales from Brittany in 1485. Richard hastened to meet him with a force twice as large and three times as untrustworthy. On Bosworth Field his force dwindled away and was beaten, and he was left fighting alone, bravely (and a little ludicrously) shouting "Treason" until he was dispatched. England's crown was plucked from a bush and placed on the head of Henry VII; the civil war was over.

By the 16th century, the twin problems of overmighty subjects and vulnerable thrones had been diminished by a threefold process of attrition, destruction, and domestication. But the situations of the English and the French nobility were not identical. The cost of lives and wealth had been much greater among the English nobility than among their French counterparts, so that, as a class, they became less distinguishable from the rest of society. By contrast, success in driving out the English had vindicated the feudal privileges of the French nobility and had seemed to justify their immunity from taxation. Since their social prestige outlasted the military occasion, the class survived—numerous, haughty, and favored—into a world where their talents were irrelevant and their privileges were parasitic.

Despite these differences, the nobility of both countries shared a common predicament: they either must adjust to changing conditions or be by-passed. Whether they knew it or not, their desperate internecine squabbles were the death rattle of feudal society.

# 3

# Italy, Germany, and the East

In the West, the formidable but vain English quest for empire ended in the formation of territorial states in which the nobility had ceased to be an independent, divisive power. The nobility had been decimated by civil strife; the gaps in their ranks had been replenished by new and loyal appointments; and hereafter, as a factor against the Crown, the nobility of the West were finished. Previously it had been the nobility who had led the effective movements of opposition against a tyrannical or inadequate monarch. Now Western monarchs had to fear their lesser gentry and bourgeois rather than their barony. The decline of the nobility as a source of opposition does not also mean the decline of the nobility in terms of place, power, and prestige. Nobility, very gradually, drew closer to the Crown and shared in the rewards of influence and the status that the court connection was coming to carry. This transition is an important watershed in the history of Europe; but it was not a pan-European phenomenon, for in the central states and in the east the conditions were different. The structure of power was more decentralized: the petty prince and the lesser nobility were the forces to contend with. In Germany, western Germany especially, the cities, merchants, and artisans were a significant social element. The great Hanseatic League of the Late Middle Ages still flourished, and continued to do so into the 17th century. With trade as their obsession, however, the groups' political importance was slight. Despite fragmentation, internally, the monarchies of the center and east were pressed for their very existences by the Ottoman Turks. While the West was able to construct a new society, the middle and eastern states of Europe were struggling to survive. To make matters worse, this mortal struggle coincided with the general European recession, and the numerous nobility found that their only way to retain their profits was to step up the process of serfdom at a time when serfdom was passing out of existence elsewhere. Europe's hinterland lay precisely where the pressures and strains upon Europe were most immediate and heavy; where feudal particularism and lack of state centralization had a longer tradition and where divisive forces ran deeper; where ethnic animosities were most bitter; and where the domination of small princes and smaller nobles had become more firmly entrenched.

Germany, sitting between the highly developed states and the borderlands of European civilization, had once envisioned herself as the heir to the Roman Empire, the bastion of civilization in a dissolving world. In this period the palm of civilization was passing to nation-states in the west and into the principalities of the south. Germany's history did not well prepare her for a place in the competition for power at this time. Her contributions to the development of the West would be immense in the realm of the spirit but, politically, she seemed to be an anachronism.

Unlike Western Europe where monarchy was giving coherent form to new nations, Germany inherited an old form from Charlemagne—the Reich. The Reich did not correspond to the area inhabited by German-speaking people; at this stage it was larger, a hollow shell within which a myriad of smaller states rattled. About 70 free cities, some unattached nobility, and more than 200 lay and ecclesiastical principalities made up the Reich or, as it came to be called in the 15th century, The Holy Roman Empire of the German nation. Its elective monarchy was a facade for old time's sake; and the Empire was a shadow of its former self. During the 14th century the power of the Emperor was little more than he could muster on his own account as a local ruler. But, theoretically, he wielded an oversuzerainty throughout Europe. The old bonds of the Empire with Italy had slackened to the extent that they were scarcely felt; and the attempts to re-assert them proved little less than farcical.

## ITALY AND THE EMPIRE

Both the plans and the failures of the Emperors in regard to Italy are germane to an understanding of the cultural changes that we call the Renaissance. Pro- and anti-Imperial factions enlivened the politics of the Italian states from the 14th to the 16th centuries. The hope (or threat) of Imperial interference long continued to be a dominant political issue. More important was the abject failure of the Emperors to extend their wills over Italy, since the freedom of Italian states from external domination was a crucial ingredient in the making of the Renaissance. Imperial pusillanimity was an indispensible precondition of Italian vitality.

Naïvely imagining that he could pacify Italy and display Imperial sovereignty, Henry VII of Luxembourg (1308-1313) crossed the Alps with a few hundred knights. With this paltry force, in the face of opposition, he was unable to reach St. Peters for a public crowning and had to be content with a crowning in secret. Then Florence closed its gates against him and, without funds, he was obliged to withdraw. He died on the way home of a fever complicated, perhaps, by humiliation.

Louis IV of Bavaria (1314-1347) took the same road and with equally bizarre results. Since Pope John XXII refused to recognize Louis' election, he had himself crowned in Rome by two excommunicated monks and four syndics, or representatives, of the people (1327). With ostentatious formality Louis deposed John and called a commission to elect another pope, "anti-Pope" Nicholas V. This unfortunate monk was soon reduced to supplicating for his life at Avignon, and Louis spent the remainder of his reign seeking a reconciliation with the papacy. Just before death, Pope John separated Italy from the Empire (1334)—this had no practical effect beyond confirming by bull what had been determined by the Alps and the ineffectiveness of Emperors long since.

Weakness, and not a national political spirit, brought about the Germanization of the Empire. Only by assiduously cultivating the Pope was Charles IV (1346-1378) able to have himself cere-monially crowned in Rome. Also, by grace of the Pope, he was able to issue a declaration of Imperial independence on his re-turn, known as the Golden Bull (1356).

Henceforward the papacy was excluded from Imperial elec-tions, but instead of strengthening the Emperor the price of this gain was a boost to local particularism: for the powers of the Electors were considerably enlarged and their several states pro-nounced indivisible.* In contrast to France, where independence advanced hand in glove with royal consolidation, the pattern of German-Imperial independence was an arrangement just short of disintegration.

One last effort was made to overawe Italy by Rupert, Count Palatine (1400-1410), and it turned into an even greater debacle than the expedition of Henry VII. Rupert had to pawn the crown to pay his way home from Lombardy.

### DISUNITY VERSUS DYNASTIC SUCCESSION

North of the Alps, the efforts of Emperors to bring their powers and functions up to a level with their office and status met with stiff resistance. The concern of the German princes, second only to extending their territories, was to enlarge their independence; and, consistent with this aim, the Electors were on guard against the establishment of any hereditary succession to the Imperial crown.

Rudolph of Hapsburg (1273-1291) had managed to wrest Aus-tria from Ottokar II of Bohemia and, having made himself a ruler of substance, he hoped to pass on the Imperial crown to his son. Perversely, the Electors turned to a weak Count Adolph of Nassau until battle suggested that Rudolph's son, Albert, was irresistible. Only then (1298) did the Electors offer him the crown. His death allowed a switch to the House of Luxembourg (Henry VII) to be followed by another shift to the House of Bavaria

---

* The College of Electors, whose form was thus defined through the 18th century, consisted of three ecclesiastics (the Archbishops of Mayence, Trier (Trèves), and Cologne) and four lay princes (the Margrave of Brandenburg, the Duke of Saxony, the Count Palatine of the Rhine, and the King of Bohemia).

(Louis IV). Henry VII had been fortunate enough to marry off his son, John the Blind, to the heiress of Bohemia. Thus his son, Charles, coming to the crown under the auspices of the Pope, owned Bohemia and Luxembourg and increased these holdings by taking over Brandenburg. Like Albert of Austria he controlled states on either side of the Empire and, not unnaturally, made every effort to ensure the election of his eldest son, Wenzel (1370-1400). Wenzel, unhappily for him, inherited only the Bohemian portion of his father's domains, which left him weak enough to be deposed and replaced by a still weaker candidate, Rupert, Count Palatine. Rupert's death caused a dispute from which Sigismund emerged triumphant. Sigismund was King of Hungary, and brother and heir of Wenzel of Bohemia. At Wenzel's death he added heresy-ridden Bohemia to Hungary and, thus equipped, hastened to provide for his succession. He married off his daughter to Albert of Hapsburg, King of Austria, and persuaded the Estates General of both Hungary and Bohemia to recognize Albert as his successor. And the Electors discreetly followed suit. From Albert's brief and insignificant reign (1438-1439), the Hapsburgs retained the hollow Imperial crown almost continuously for five centuries.

Marriage and the sword had been the weapons by which this great power was established on the corner of the Empire. Austria and Hungary dominated the Danube, and Bohemia thrust northward into the heart of the confederation. But, for the moment, this amalgamation was premature—a sneak preview of things to come—for Albert left only a posthumous child and Bohemia entrusted itself to the care of its Hussite leader while Hungary turned to a gifted military family for protection against the Turks. Eventually, both gravitated to the King of Poland with whose family Frederick of Hapsburg, ruler of Austria, arranged judicious marriages. Only after the Turks annihilated the combined Czech and Hungarian forces and their king at Mohács (1526) did the Estates offer Frederick their dual crown. Having amassed this conglomerate kingdom, the surprising thing is that the Hapsburgs never threatened to swallow the rest of Germany. One reason was that their kingdom was the outcome of an eastward orientation that still continued. Then the advance of the Turks not only challenged and obstructed their drive to the east but forced Hungary and Austria to fight for their very existence. Moreover, the Reformation introduced one more division into Germany, which prohibited unity while religious zeal was rampant. In any event, the Hapsburgs were not a self-conscious German power but were a dynasty whose holdings were strung from the North Sea to the Carpathian Mountains. Therefore, by interest and temper they were a self-consciously cosmopolitan power opposed to national strivings.

The Electors, for so long chary of lineal succession, finally yielded to Hapsburg power, but the peculiar preoccupations of that dynasty permitted localism to flourish unchecked within the Empire. Although at first glance, the interests of dynasty and principality seemed opposed, actually the rivals realized their objectives—both contenders won trophies.

### THE EAST

A cardinal fact of German history is Germany's lack of natural frontiers. Germans are but one of many groups of peoples sustained by the North and Eastern European Plain. Stretching from the North Sea to the Urals and the Russian Steppes and spreading east of the Carpathians both northward and southward to the Baltic and Black Seas, this great Plain offers its peoples no shelter from the incursions of their neighbours. Indeed, the very flatness of the Plain has encouraged aggressive drives by the Germans against the Slavs and counterdrives by Slavs against Germans, and there is no love lost between them. A generation ago under Hitler, German conquests had reached a front stretching between Leningrad and Stalingrad, within 40 miles of Moscow itself. Today fortunes are reversed, and the Communism of the East surrounds and partly encompasses Berlin. From the perspective of centuries Nazism and Communism are recent phenomena, while the thrusts and counterthrusts of the peoples of the Plain are probably as old as its habitation.

Hence, particularly, the history of Poland-Lithuania is one of constantly changing, undulating frontiers. These Slavic peoples originally were similar to the Bulgars, Serbs, Croats, and Slovenes to the South. But this broad Slavic belt from the Adriatic to the Baltic was broken by Finnish-Asiatic invaders, called *magyars,* who swept up the Danube and settled in its basin within the circle of the Carpathian mountains. These Hungarians were not Slavs; they cut off the northern Slavs from the South and from Byzantium and, since their own ties grew stronger with the West (by river) than with the South, they became Roman Catholic rather than Greek Orthodox in the 11th century. As a result of Hungarian settlement, the Poles and Czechs (Bohemia) lost contact with Orthodoxy and also turned Catholic. Farther East, the Slavic-Finns or Russians had been Christianized earlier than the Poles, in the 10th century, when their relations with Constantinople were still quite vigorous. But, since then, the Mongols had come between Moscow and Constantinople; indeed Batu, the grandson of Genghis Khan, had extended Mongol dominion beyond the banks of the Dnieper River, capturing both Moscow and Kiev by 1340. A century later the Golden Horde (so called because of the riches they gathered from tribute) were Mohammedans. Nevertheless, the Russians remained Orthodox. While Orthodoxy linked them to the Balkan Slavs from whom they were separated geographically, it divided them from the Northern Slavs with whom they were contiguous. Thus, in large measure, Russia's isolation from Europe was a spiritual isolation, and has been considered so ever since.

SOCIAL STRUCTURE

Russia, Poland, Bohemia, and Hungary present social patterns unlike the feudalism that was so highly developed by Normandy. Although in Russia and Lithuania smaller gentry were tenured and owed military service, the nobility everywhere were independent freeholders, owing no obligations and bound only voluntarily to their prince by a mutual interest in security and good order. Beneath these free nobility were lesser gentry, the petty artisans of the village, and peasantry ranging from the virtual freeholder to the bondsman and landless laborer. There was no numerous native middle class. Mongol invasions had destroyed the prosperity of Kievan Russia and the indigenous merchant class disappeared; in Hungary, Poland, and Bohemia the local peoples did not venture away from agriculture. So, in all countries, trade was carried on by immigrants, mostly Germans, who formed foreign and unassimilable colonies in the major cities. These German bourgeois found themselves competing with Jews who were arriving in numbers, especially to Poland, because they had been deported from Western Europe. In 1290 Edward I had expelled the Jews from England. Phillip the Fair followed suit in France in 1306. German nobility and townsfolk drove many out by terror and intimidation during the 14th century and Ferdinand and Isabella banned them from Spain in 1492. As newcomers and as urban dwellers, they aroused the hostility of the native rural populations; also, by competing, they intensified the bitterness with which the German bourgeoisie already regarded them. Until Israel became a state in 1947 no sanctuary has spared Jews from bigotry and intolerance.

Both the independence of the nobility and the absence of an indigenous' bourgeois distinguish Eastern from Western Europe. Even more important was the resurgence of serfdom in the East, and for the very same reasons that it was fast disappearing in the West—increased desire of profit. The West found it more profitable to permit the serf to buy his way to freedom by leasing either land or labor as a landless wage earner. The catalyst, of course, was the availability of money: money relations gradually replaced personal relations. But in the East bullion was scarce, although the desire to exploit it had not abated. In fact the desire had increased; landowners were trying to increase demesne production at the expense of the peasant, but without ready cash the serf could not bargain his way to freedom, nor could the landowner conveniently pay wages. The easiest way to farm for profit seemed to be to reduce the lesser peasantry and the landless laborers to servile status. The acquisitive spirit can run in many channels; in the West it worked for a free labor force; in the East it increased the numbers of men in bondage. The Bohemian nobility, for instance, took advantage of the Hussite wars to impose their demands on their tenants; the Hungarian nobility depressed incoming Roumanians who were fleeing up the Danube from the Turks. In Prussia, Russia, and Poland, the landed classes used governmental power to fix workers to the soil. This curious process of capitalistic farming, coupling itself with an immobile and servile labor force, reached its zenith in the 17th century but it began in the 15th century. On one side of Europe, higher productivity accompanied emancipation; on the other side, efficiency was achieved at the cost of social regression. Ruthlessness and a disregard for human freedom proved the most effective means to success, and the impact of this lesson on political and social mores East of the Elbe is only now being effaced.

## THE TIDES OF EASTERN INVASIONS

During the 14th and 15th centuries the warriors of Asia and Asia Minor penetrated deeper into Europe than they had ever done before. And yet, by 1492, Spain had turned from domestic disputes to rid herself once and for all of the Moors of Granada. The East, however, was more vulnerable than the West. As we have seen, the Mongols used their extraordinary equestrian skills to conquer the whole of Russia and hold it for ransom. So long as tribute was paid, the existing administrations were not disturbed. It was under these conditions that Muscovy made itself chief among the subject principalities. Ivan (John) I (1328-1340) played the part of the obsequious and dutiful servant so well that he was confirmed as the Grand Prince of Russia and his son was given sovereignty over all other princes except, of course, the Khan. Ivan's nickname "moneybag" reveals the reason for his preferential treatment: he was the Tartars' tribute collector.

This service to those above brought Ivan and his successors immunity from invasion and also extensive power over their rivals below. Moscow's power and peace soon attracted the Metropolitan of the Church, and the city's importance was enhanced by its becoming the center of ecclesiastical administration. Preservation of the Church depended on preservation of Moscow. Only the growth of Muscovy could cast out the Islamic Horde, so the Church was extravagant in its spiritual blessings and theoretical elevation of the Prince of Muscovy, and the Church joined wholeheartedly with the state to establish local absolutism.

Three facts disturbed the steady accumulation of power and property by Moscow. A child heir set in motion the familiar bloody struggle for the succession; at the same time the old policy of obedience to the Khan was abandoned because the long period of consolidation had renewed confidence; and yet another world conqueror from Mongolia, called Tamerlane the Great, had arisen to command all the lands between Manchuria and the Caspian Sea. Tamerlane did not bother to enter Russia until one of his underlings rebelled in 1395. Up to this time Muscovy had met with mixed success in monster battles and had managed only to reduce its tribute payments. Tamerlane took the Volga basin but was diverted southward to tackle the Turks. He ravaged Mesopotamia—it has never recovered—then, in 1402, inflicted a crushing defeat on the Turks at Angora. For a moment Tamerlane had diverted Turkey from Europe and, in so doing, had postponed the fall of Constantinople. If he had lived the Asian conqueror might have wrestled with Turkey and Muscovy, and Europe might have been left to its own devices. But Tamerlane died and his work died with him (1405).

Muscovy remained a Tartar tributary, but continued to spar unceasingly with the overlords. She simultaneously imposed her own dominance on Tver to the west and Novgorod to the northwest and made inroads southwest into Lithuania. Finally, in 1480, the tribute was refused and, though terrible vengeance was threatened, it was not taken: the Khanate had simply withdrawn. These signal successes and strokes of luck came under Ivan (John) III (1462-1505) and his wife Sophia. Sophia was the niece of the last of the Byzantine emperors, Constantine XI, who died honorably in the siege of Constantinople (1453). Constantinople's fall —the last vestige of the ancient Roman Empire—left Moscow as the guardian of the Orthodox faith. The city claimed to be the third Rome, replacing the two that had fallen to heresy: Rome to Catholicism and now Constantinople to Mohammedanism. "The third Rome, Moscow, stands and a fourth there will not be." It was a fitting slogan for a new empire spreading from the Urals to the Gulf of Finland, from the White Sea almost to Kiev —now set upon the path of greatness. The modern form of Eastern Europe was taking shape.

When the Mongols were overrunning Russia in the first decades of the 14th century, only pagan Lithuania had had the strength to force them back and to win frontage on the Black Sea. Meanwhile, at Lithuania's other extremity, the Teutonic Order had been battering against her and against Poland from the Baltic Sea. Whenever Lithuania pressed east the Order would advance, whenever Poland and Lithuania turned back together to deal with the Order the Turks or the Muscovites would take this opportunity to tear strips from their southeastern and eastern frontiers.

Poland and Lithuania labored under disadvantages. Not only did they sprawl across the no-man's land of the European Plain but the strength and independence of their nobility made it impossible for a strong centralized monarchy of the Western type to emerge. The best that could be established, after the conversion and marriage of Jagiello to the Polish heiress (1386), was a loose dynastic federation of the two states. Yet if the monarchy was weakened institutionally by a diffusion of power, it was strengthened militarily by the common hatred of Poles and Lithuanians for the Teutonic Order. Jagiello smashed them at Grunwald (near Tannenberg) in 1410 but they recovered and had to be reduced again in a 13-year war. This time (1466) Poland demanded homage for East Prussia and incorporated Pomerania, the mouth of the Vistula and the Danzig. But having gained this access to the Baltic, Poland and Lithuania lost their frontiers on the Black Sea to the Turks.

### THE MOHAMMEDAN ADVANCE

This remarkable heathen invasion of Europe, the longest to date, was prepared in advance by the depredations of Christian powers in the Byzantine Empire. The Fourth Crusade, profiting Venice and Genoa, destroyed the commerce of Byzantium and, in so doing, sealed it irrevocably from the West for its Orthodoxy already insulated it spiritually. Driven partly by the Mongols and lured by the patent weakness of Byzantium, the Turks captured all the lands held by the Empire in Asia Minor by 1330. There was no stopping them. The resplendent army of knights, led by Emperor Sigismund and John the Fearless of Burgundy, were no match for the religious zeal and disconcertingly unchivalrous tactics of the invader (Nicopolis fell in 1396). By 1400 the whole of the Balkans to the Danube was Turkish preserve.

Bajazet (1389-1403) had just begun the siege of Constantinople when Tamerlane and his horde poured into Asia Minor. Tamerlane proved invincible (Angora 1402) but the torrent ebbed as swiftly as it had flowed. Suleiman (1403-1410), son of Bajazet, cut his losses, making harmless treaties with the Emperor and lifting his tribute from the Greeks and Serbs, so that he was free to revive his people. In the following generation all Turkey's earlier conquests were reconquered and more land was gained despite heroic opposition in Albania and Hungary. Once again the Ottomans encircled Constantinople and, this time, there was no salvation. It fell to Mohammed II (1451-1481) in 1453. The ancient church of St. Sophia became a mosque. There had not been such pillage, rapine, and murder in the city since the Fourth Crusade. For the moment, Turkey's appetite was sated; the capitol of the Empire was moved from Asia Minor to Europe (Adrianople) and these astonishing gains were consolidated. Then, under Selim the Grim (1512-1520), the flame of conquest was rekindled. Selim circled the shores of the Black Sea and placed the Crimean Tartars under tribute. Then he turned south to the Aegean and besieged Rhodes, but died of plague. It was left to Suleiman the Magnificent to take Rhodes (1522), and he also overcame Belgrade (1521), which opened up the Danube plain to him. In 1526 a total of 30,000 Czechs and Hungarians threw themselves, in desperation, on 100,000 Turks and perished (1526). This battle at Mohács, just south of Buda, made Buda the advance post of Islam. Sickness and foul weather spared Vienna in 1529 from the same fate as Belgrade and Buda; Suleiman seemed happy to leave the Hapsburgs' thin slice of western and northern Hungary for comfort.

Turkish rule was harsh but tolerant. Many homeless Jews found shelter in central Asia Minor. Perhaps the most abhorrent feature of Turkish rule, to the modern mind, is that persons as well as purses were liable for levy. The most beautiful girls were drafted for service in the harem; and the most strapping youngsters were taken for conversion to Islam and exclusive military service. In fact, Christian families competed to have their children impressed, for to serve the Sultan was to tread the avenue of possible advancement; much might be gained for the loss of a soul.

Turkey spread into Europe in three stages: beginning in the second half of the 14th century, again during the half century after recovery from Tamerlane's destructions; and finally in the first three decades of the 16th century. Except for the inadequate effort of Emperor Sigismund, the defense of Europe was left to those immediately threatened. There was no massive crusade, for neither states nor peoples were interested. Pius II (1458-1564), who had set his heart on a crusade, was gratified on his death bed to see a few shiploads of crusaders sail out from Venice, but as soon as the fleet learned that the Pope was dead it promptly came about and returned home. Idealism for the Catholic cause was faint: religious zeal was absorbed by reform movements in every period of Ottoman advance. Fundamentally, Europe was unconcerned; the vision of a universal Christian community was an unremembered dream; recession, hard times, social problems, the convulsions of dying feudalism, and the birth pangs of centralized monarchy preoccupied the states and peoples of the West. The Turks succeeded for the lack of a concerted opposition. At first apprehensive, Europe came to tolerate and even to countenance Ottoman power as it declined. After all, by standing astride the eastern Mediterranean in a belligerent posture the heathens confirmed the West in its independent course of global oceanic expansion westward. Eastern Europe's loss determined Western Europe's destiny.

# 4

# The Culture of the Renaissance

The common use of the term Renaissance to mean the cultural developments in Europe from the 14th to the 16th centuries is hazardous. For one thing, the word does not fit the facts very closely and, for another, it distinguishes one period too sharply from another. The word is too small and neat for the period. Coined by the Italian artist and art historian Vasari to applaud the return of classical excellence—*rinascita* means a rebirth—the term was taken up by later French historians and given a more general application. This was perhaps unfortunate, for even within the limited ambit of art and architecture the idea of a sudden rebirth was partly a myth and a delusion. The concept, however, has won security of tenure by long usage and cannot be dislodged. Because it seems to lend special glamor to a particular time span and to play favorites with eras, it has offended some sensibilities. Historians have seen a Renaissance in the 12th and 13th centuries, and they see maturer expressions of 15th-century trends in the 16th and 17th centuries. This is not surprising, for Clio, the muse of history, knows no periods.

In the past, when history was conceived of primarily as cultural and political history, and when historians took the humanists' notion of their own originality at face value, it was possible for some scholars to reduce the period to a few quintessentials: the rediscovery of man and the world; a renewed sense of joy in life;

asceticism and symbolism giving way to sensuousness and naturalism; realism replacing idealism; and experimentation in the pursuit of knowledge displacing traditionalism and obscurantism.

To a degree, all of these formulas are correct, but they emphasize change at the expense of continuity. "Restless youth and crabbed age" do always live together, and new departures were shaped by old concerns and only gradually replaced them. In architecture the concept of a Renaissance veils the wonderful resilience of Gothic style in northern Europe. In England, for instance, there remain majestic monuments of Perpendicular Gothic from the 16th century, including the ethereal splendor of King's College Chapel, Cambridge, the fabric of which (but for windows, choir screen, and organ) was completed in 1515. Often Renaissance historians underestimated the change and vitality of the Middle Ages, and naïvely equated the novel features of the Renaissance with the good, and the rest as husk that had to be outgrown before the world could come of age. Some scholars, disenchanted with the holocausts of modern Europe, have been less sanguine about the Renaissance. From the outset, they accept the period as a complex one. They view it as a period full of ambivalences; a period with a checkered moral legacy.

The previous chapters suggested that the unifying forces of the Late Middle Ages had been seriously weakened, and that new movements and institutions were bringing internal wars and social dislocation in their trains. At the same time, retrenchment and the specter of Ottoman invasion cast a gloom which makes the achievement of Renaissance humanists all the more remarkable, almost perverse. They remained optimistic about human nature and the possibilities of human reason, despite much of the evidence; they offered a set of secular and cultural values that threatened to replace the power of the papacy as a unifying factor until the Reformation sundered Europe spiritually forever; above all, they generated and disseminated an enthusiasm for "new learning" which, in spirit if not in form, is still alive.

Theirs was a remarkable achievement—a pan-European culture and style that were won by sheer intellectual virtuosity despite the social and political tensions and the setbacks of the period. It is this virtuosity, one supposes, that tempts historians to try to sum up all developments in a few pithy phrases. Even if one could capsulate the Renaissance in pungent phrases, the more profound question would remain unanswered: What was the relationship between cultural changes and their social and political *milieux?* From one vantage point, cultural change may seem to be a mere reflection of social and other changes: for instance, the mounting chorus of applause for intellectual cultivation over more purely spiritual ends seems to arise directly from an increasingly sophisticated scholasticism; the change mirrors burgeoning universities, the vitality of cities, the emergence of secular patrons, and the crises that underscored the worth of sheer physical existence. On the other hand, some developments belie this simple metaphor: everywhere diversity was filling the breaches in the cosmopolitan institutions and ideals of the past, yet Renaissance men were committing themselves to a search for new universal values. There is surely a reaching back—an element of reaction to their environment—in this process. This suggests that a culture can grow and flourish in and also stand apart from its context. It may even stand in judgment on its context. As a modern writer says of Goethe, genius is both representative and unrepresentative of its age. His saying could be applied to the diverse talents, esoteric cults, and intellectual movements that enrich the Renaissance era. The problem of tracing relationships—capable of a dazzling variety of answers—may founder on the complexities of reality. Indeed, separating culture from context is rather artificial; but doing so may further understanding.

### THE SETTING

As the old sense of universalism was departing, in its stead had grown a new awareness of diversity: there were new focuses for popular allegiance. In Western Europe the nation-state was becoming the focus of strong loyalties: France and England were born as nations in the travail of the Hundred Years War; the unity of Spain was cemented by the marriage of Ferdinand of Aragon to Isabella of Castile in 1469, and this pair completed their wedding pact by driving the Moslem Moors from their last foothold in Granada in 1492. To the north the Scandinavian countries had accepted a union under the Crown of Sweden, which had lasted for a sufficient time to break the chronic habit of local baronial warfare.

The many small states of Germany and Italy remained exceptions to the national rule, but they also shared the urge to develop strong communal loyalties. Although they were dwarfed by the giants to the West, they were nevertheless states with all the appurtenances and apparatus of statehood—diplomatic corps, networks of alliances, civil servants, and forces to command. Their local loyalties were equally if not more fully developed than national feelings.

In Italy the stronger cities managed to maintain a measure of independence but, by a process of large eating small, only seven major states existed by the end of the 15th century. The Kingdom of Naples, long disputed territory between the Houses of Anjou and Aragon, finally fell to Aragon in 1435, and Aragon also controlled Sicily. Spain thus came to control the southern half of the peninsula. Acting as a buffer between the feudal south and the commercial north, the papal states joined Adriatic Sea to Mediterranean. This loose conglomeration of cities and principalities was jostled from the north by the Duchy of Ferrara and the Republics of Florence and Siena. These, with the Duchies of Mantua and Modena, were the smaller principalities, Florence being dominant among them. All were flanked to the north by the larger holdings of the Dukes of Savoy, by Milan, and by the Venetian Republic.

It was in the north of Italy, among the furious world of little states that the Renaissance first flourished. The northern states were neither feudal nor puppets; they were independent, and the most vital of them were republics. Since 1311 Milan, had been ruled by despots of the Visconti family, whose male line died out in 1447. Sovereignty then reverted to the republic, until an upstart condottiero, Francesco Sforza, made himself Duke by starving the city into submission. Ferrara was governed by the Este family, and Mantua was governed by the Gonzagas. The papal states were never fully subjected to the papacy until the reign of that most immoral of popes, the Borgia, Alexander VI (1492-1503), whose son, Caesare, undertook a ruthless extortion of obedience from the surrounding principalities. His project was completed by "the warrior pope," Julius II, who left his successor, the Medici Leo X, a measure of stability and wealth sufficient to retain such talents as Michelangelo's and Raphael's to adorn Rome.

Florence, Venice, and Siena were the outstanding republics, but a Renaissance republic should not be confused with a democracy. Siena was an oligarchy; the Medici family, by virtue of their wealth from banking and their constitutional astuteness, managed to dominate Florence's Councils. Venice, though it boasted a complex constitution of checks and balances, never pretended to be anything other than a mercantile oligarchy.

The first manifestations of the Renaissance are generally acknowledged to be Florentine. During the consolidation of the republican oligarchy, after the early 1380's, Florence found itself encircled and isolated by the conquests of the Duke of Milan. This threat distilled among Florentines an awareness both of their political danger and of the virtues that their republican system embodied. Its origins could be traced back to the ancient communes of Italy before the rise of the Roman Empire. By exploring their special heritage, Florentines generated public pride and self-consciousness, and came to value and extol civic-mindedness in all pursuits, whether art or commerce, scholarship or government. In time, these attitudes spread far beyond Florence. When, for instance, Venice felt itself to be the last outpost of Republicanism, in 16th-century Italy, then we find her artists and architects adorning her beauty. Self-awareness and a sense of individuality would seem to have been important factors.

Venice had always been more stable than the other Italian states; and though this stability was often credited to her constitution, it owed more to the uniform seafaring interests of her peoples and to the relatively invulnerable position of the island capital. On the mainland, not only was state pitted against state but also class warred against class. Lesser guilds clamored for power against greater guilds and, cutting through all these squabbles, Guelphs campaigned against Ghibellines. Ghibellines were those who favored and relied on the old Imperial connection, and Guelphs were those who were opposed to that link and who looked to the papacy for support. Northern Italy offered the stimulating prospect of endless turmoil and incessant commotion.

If this lusty independence was a breeding ground of the Renaissance, it is also true that the Renaissance was an urban phenomenon. The bustle of the city included the busy hum of commerce. While it is true that the middle class was proliferating, the period was one of considerable dislocation, of closing of frontiers, and of limited surpluses, especially in Northern Europe. Some bourgeois were declining, particularly those whose fortunes were tied up in the woollen guilds. In England, on the other hand, the export of wool cloth was increasingly profitable. Guilds, as such, however, both in England and Italy, were slowly losing influence in society at large as they lost control of their own members. Throughout the period the guilds fought a defensive battle to supervise the standards of production and to oversee wages, prices, and the conditions of apprenticeship. A market system and market values were making breaches through their older restrictive practices. Individual and joint stock ventures had become the high roads to wealth traveled by a minority. Banking, trading, the exploitation of mines and forests, the holding of a concession here and a monopoly there, all these were still fields of promise provided that one streamlined operations and supervised every detail of business with the utmost rigor—in the style of a Jacob Fugger. Even so, a fabulous fortune could be dissipated by bad luck or political miscalculation.

For classes below the bourgeoisie the pattern was similar. An artisan, breaking from the guild and manning his own shop, might profit; another less venturous craftsman might not. In this period the petit bourgeois began to form as a class with an uncertain future. By and large, small farmers, copyholders,* and tenants improved their real standards of living. Serfdom began to disappear in the West, although East of the Elb it revived with an even greater intensity of exploitation than earlier. The Renaissance took shallower root in Eastern Europe, for it thrived in an economic environment that was at once rapacious and ebullient.

The Renaissance was indebted to another social transforma-

---

* Copyholders were neither freeholders nor leaseholders, but were people who enjoyed the use of land for certain terms of years in return for prescribed services, all of which were recorded on a copy kept in the manor court.

tion: the pacification of the nobility. Pacification is not the same thing as decline; nobility adjusted themselves surprisingly well to new conditions. Of course, this pacification advanced fitfully and varied from area to area. In Italy the process occurred earlier than in France and England. Swords were never beaten into plowshares, but they were used less frequently in battle and more decoratively as emblems of rank. The brooding castle was abandoned for a fortified manor house; and the house, in turn, was exchanged for a town or a country dwelling. And as this occurred, music, art, and literature found an ever-growing and appreciative audience among the aristocracy.

The seeking out of patrons became an art in itself with flattery as its attendant vice. Men of second rank had to attach themselves to a patron to survive. Only the greatest scholars and artists could afford the luxury of unbridled individualism. Patronage continued to be wielded by the guilds, but the significant change was the emancipation of the artist from the guild because of an expanding market elsewhere. Private individuals and heads of state were investing in culture for themselves, and lavishly. So church patronage, though still prodigious, faced rich and powerful secular rivals.

RENAISSANCE HUMANISM

Art, letters, philosophy, science, and music freed themselves increasingly from the tutelage of the church, matching the steady growth (from the 13th century) of court and individual lay patronage. Indeed, the church found itself drawn willy-nilly into the wake of new intellectual fashions that it had not prescribed. The spectacle of Gregory VII with an Emperor (Henry IV) at his knees in the snow begging him for forgiveness in 1076 was quite different from that of Julius II (in 1506) hoping that Michelangelo would not leave Rome after a tiff. Speculation and scholarship had once been the virtual monopoly of the Church; now popes and bishops were patron-pupils of the Renaissance. Laymen crowded clergy at the fountains of knowledge and the Renaissance saw the quickening of a process that is still occurring: the laicization of culture.

This bold departure—the founding and development of a

nonclerical intellectual aristocracy—was fortified by the authority of the past, especially in Italy where the remains of ancient Rome were still to be seen. The classical (sometimes misleadingly called the pagan) revival was a primary and original impetus for changes in intellectual manners, and it remained a constant influence throughout this period. Antiquity gave legitimacy to the secular pursuits of the Renaissance. It offered a treasury of literature, art, architecture, jurisprudence, philosophy, and science— all of which to the Renaissance mind had been inadequately appreciated in the past. The Renaissance was, indeed, unfair to the Middle Ages; it overestimated its own achievement and underestimated the fervor and vitality of the earlier period. It scoffed at medieval enslavement to tradition but, in abandoning one authority, the Renaissance was quick to substitute another; the distant past was venerated because its prestige shed security on the secular invasion of hidden mysteries. As a layman venturing to write a cosmic epic—*The Divine Comedy*—Dante (1265-1321) was comforted by the companionship of Virgil in his journey to the other world. Yet antiquity was more than a brace and a touchstone of legitimacy. It was an ideal, a source of inspiration, and sometimes an obstruction. Possibly Leonardo da Vinci (1452-1519) might have discovered the circulation of the blood if Galen's theory of invisible pores in the wall of the heart had not inhibited him.

The rediscovery of classical Latin style and its imitation were preconditions of Renaissance success. Classical usage symbolized, by discarding scholastic Latin, an improvement on the whole scholastic tradition; pure classical Latin became the universal language through which the Renaissance could exert its utmost influence. Moreover, in elegance and precision it well suited the courtly patronage that sustained the humanists.

The consideration of antiquity also encouraged the use of vernacular, since Latin and Greek, in their day, had been vulgar tongues. Actually, the formation of vernacular speech began far back in the Middle Ages; what was novel was that the humanists dignified local dialects by employing them in their finest works. Dante, Petrarch (1304-1374), and Boccaccio (1313-1375), devout classicists as they were, helped to make their native Tuscan the language of Italy by giving it shape and beauty. The use of vernacular also accompanied the growing sense of national identity. Thus the patriot-heretic Wycliffe (about 1320-1384), wrote vigorous and balanced English prose, which Chaucer (about 1340-1400) simplified and smoothed in preparation for the splendor of the Elizabethan era. In France, Rabelais (about 1495-1553) followed in the footsteps of irreverent troubadours and poets who sang and rhymed in vernacular; and Cervantes (1547-1616) performed a similar service for Spain.

In the short run the revival of classical Latin served the humanists', élitist purpose well enough, but in the long run it is clear that they killed a vital, living language in order to revive a dead thing. In patronizing the vernacular tongues, however, the Renaissance laid the basis for mass national literacy and the mass secular culture that is now in being.

Strictly speaking, humanists were scholars of the classics but, in the broader, Ciceronian sense, *humanitas* meant a literary refinement and a mental cultivation that went far beyond mere academic discipline. In the fullest sense it amounted to an attitude toward life, to a fresh view of man's place in the cosmos, and to a substantial reassessment of his scale of values. Whereas the saint, the ascetic, or the chivalrous knight formerly had been ideal types, now homage was paid to the prince and the courtier. Castiglione's (1478-1529) *The Courtier* idealized the man of affairs with a quiver-full of accomplishments, devoted to his prince. This courtier was expected to have mastered etiquette and the classics. He should possess every grace; he should spice every conversation with wit, and should give honest counsel to the prince under the spur of his strong sense of civic duty. He was also expected to be a hardy warrior. Few men approximated to this ideal. Michelangelo (1475-1564) was no courtier; Leonardo was too preoccupied with his experiments to be a man of affairs. Benvenuto Cellini (1500-1571) was half genius and half undisciplined adolescent, and Sir Walter Raleigh (about 1552-1618) the Elizabethan sea-dog and courtier, was deficient in emotional balance though not in talents. If no one was perfect, there were plenty of men who were jacks of many trades and masters of them too. The specialization of functions, characteristic of both modern and medieval society, did not then exist, and distrust between the humanities and science was not yet abroad.

So persuasive was the ideal of "the Renaissance man" that new schools sprang up exemplifying a novel philosophy of education. Vittorini da Feltre (1378-1446) hoped to produce able, graceful, cultivated dilettanti by steeping them in an all-round curriculum centered on the classics. In general, Western European education followed that pattern until this century, and the ideal of the good "all-rounder" still has currency in English private schools. American universities still follow the pattern, if not the spirit, with American history and the history of Western Civilization rather than the classics forming the core of the liberal-arts programs.

Undoubtedly the self-conscious cultivation of the classics led the humanists to an awareness of history. At first they were obsessed with fame—fame of the past and fame of the self. Among early humanists, Boccaccio wrote of the fame (and also, rather lovingly, of the infamy) of ancient women. Petrarch addressed moving epistles to posterity. After all, had not the Roman poet, Horace, predicted that he would grow great in the praise of posterity? Giorgio Vasari (1511-1574) was sufficiently aware of posterity to leave us his *Lives of the Painters, Sculptors and Architects,* which included a long sketch of himself. It was only a short step from an appreciation of one's own and others' lasting glory to a sense of history.

For the first time since antiquity, observers of affairs began to write critical secular history that avoided supernatural theories of causation and attempted to be trustworthy with the facts. Phillip de Commynes (about 1447-1511), the Flemish adviser to Louis XI, was the earliest to use his intimate knowledge of royal policy to describe and analyze in detail the crucial reign that consolidated France in the waning of the Hundred Years War. Guicciardini (1483-1540) and Machiavelli (1469-1527), both Florentines, carried Commyne's secular beginning still further in their histories of Florence.

If Guicciardini was pessimistic, Machiavelli plumbed the very depths of cynicism. His *The Prince* was an amoral handbook on how to succeed in political business. One historian, taking a lead from Machiavelli's saucy play *Mandragola,* reads it as a satire; others view it as the last resort of a republican patriot whose hopes of a united Italy were threatened by foreign warriors. Yet another resolves the incompatibility between *The Prince* and

Machiavelli's avowed republicanism by reference to his cyclical theory of constitutional change, drawn from Polybius. The anarchy that was then current could only be followed by rule of a single person. This would fit *The Prince* into a theory of historical inevitability where the causes of change lie—barring accidents or fate—in the nature of man and political society. Whatever the case, Machiavelli's secular analyses, so naked and unashamed, shocked contemporaries. With Machiavelli, the study of politics as well as history shed their religious coverings, and politics became an autonomous and self-justifying art.

Part and parcel of the secular historical method was a critical approach to sources. This had long been an important aspect of the humanists' work in gathering and collating manuscripts, and one of them, Lorenzo Valla (about 1407-1457), won a responding victory for source criticism by proving that the anachronisms in the Donation of Constantine rendered it impossible that it could have been written in the 5th century A.D. Rome's claim to dominion over surrounding lands by gift of the Emperor Constantine was based on a fraud. Not that the revelation altered the political realities at all, but the skill and cogency of Valla's demonstration eminently qualified it to be a model for subsequent analysis.

Some scholars believe that the humanists' critical approach to sources was their major lasting achievement. It was, of course, the beginning of the source and form criticism of today. But one can exaggerate the humanists' accomplishments. Although Erasmus (about 1466-1536) had a 10th-century manuscript to use for his Greek Testament, he made little use of it because it differed more than his other and later manuscripts did from *The Vulgate*. And, when Beza made his translation (in 1589), he had both a 5th- and a 6th-century manuscript, but he made little use of them because they differed widely from Erasmus' text! Still, if Renaissance criticism was less than thoroughgoing, it made, at least, a start.

Much of the critical work of the Renaissance was destructive; much of it took the form of satire. Erasmus learned that ridicule was as effective a method as argument in undermining rival positions, and in numerous works, most notably in the *Praise of Folly,* he slashed at the foibles and intellectual fads of past and present generations with a sharp quill. Folly, he showed, had more sense than indulgence in the antics of apparently wise men. *Letters of Obscure Men,* written by a supporter of the Hebrew scholar Reuchlin (1455-1522), was another such piece. Purporting to favor those who would repress Hebrew books, the letters pilloried crass ignorance and superstition in doing so.

Lowly priests, monks, and friars were particularly the butt of humanist barbs, for these were the purveyors of outmoded values. They, too, were the most vulnerable objects of scorn, living close to the people and to mundane temptations yet professing purity and owning special privileges. From a humanist's point of view, they shared the defects of their ecclesiastical betters and lacked their virtues. They were often mercenary and corrupt and, with it, were unlettered and unprodigal in the cause of learning. One might gather from Boccaccio's *Decameron* that priests and friars were not to be trusted with women (married or unmarried) and that monasteries and nunneries were sinks of profligacy. The Renaissance publicized its abiding anticlericalism in ribaldry and mordant humor.

Just as vernacular had been introduced by humanists to high culture, so the salacity and earthy wit of lower social orders was admitted into sophisticated usage. Happily Chaucer, though a court official, was close enough to village life to appreciate its bucolic belly laughter. Thus the "Miller's Story" in *Canterbury Tales* is pure and unadulterated smut at its most incongruous level. The wild bawdiness of Rabelais' *Garguantua and Pantagruel* is more learned, though of the same social origin.

If the humanists were abrasively anticlerical, they were not irreligious; quite the contrary: since one of their dearest pretensions was to instruct society (including the Church) in true morality. And if the virtue recommended by Machiavelli was not that of most of the humanists, his pretension was the same. Nowhere does the long retreat of the Church's influence show more clearly than here. In a vacuum of moral leadership the humanists became the formulators and the guardians of standards of right; even their attacks on the clergy were possessed with conviction as to what ought to be. Chaucer's Pardoner in *Canterbury Tales,* for instance, was a despicable hypocrite who peddled fake promises, preying for money on the superstitions of the poor and ignorant. On the one hand, this tale was an indictment of the falsity that had crept into the Church and, on the other, through it, Chaucer launched a plea for purer faith and practice.

It was in this evangelical spirit of restoring purity that some of the finest scholarly work was done in biblical studies: the German, Reuchlin, interpreted the Old Testament and the Frenchman, Lefèvre d'Etaples (about 1455-1536), interpreted the New Testament from a fresh standpoint. Erasmus lavished years of labor on his Greek New Testament in an attempt to present a text that was scrupulously accurate and in the original language.

Erasmus' particular interests owed something to the encouragement of Colet (1466-1519) and More (1478-1535) whom he met in England. Colet inspired men by his gentle personality. More inspired them by his ability and, to this day, by his *Utopia* which is still read by idealists and critics of societies' evils. Erasmus, because of his unsurpassed style, his wit, and his knowledge, became the most renowned scholar of his generation. His *Paraphrases* were recommended to English churches; his Greek New Testament became a source for later vernacular translations of the Bible. He was, for a time, the moral leader of Europe. Educated in the Netherlands by the Brethren of the Common Life—a mystic pietist order—his teaching avoided their mysticism (for he was a rationalist) and emphasized piety. He called for a return to apostolic simplicity, for forbearance and mutual understanding, and for lives to be lived by a Christ-like ethic. By criticizing the failings of the Church he inadvertently fed the fires of religious dissension and, in the heat of the Reformation, he found his former influence turning to ashes and all that he had worked for melting away. Just before the conflagration, however, he congratulated Leo X (1513-1521) on what he had done to restore piety and erudition in the Church. The humanist was instructing and encouraging the Pope.

As far as erudition was concerned, this was not always necessary. Aeneas Silvius Piccolomini was a scholar in his own right before he became Pius II (1458-1464). He was typical of Renaissance popes who patronized art and learning freely and who spent more energy consolidating their power than in improving the spiritual state of the Church.

Five popes before Pius II had employed Poggio Bracciolini (1380-1459), a supersleuth in discovering ancient manuscripts and, through men like Poggio, thousands of Greek and Roman manuscripts were preserved from destruction by men or from decay by way of time. Boccaccio once wept when he saw the state of the manuscripts in the Benedictine monastery of Monte Casino. We owe an incalculable debt to the humanists for their feverish hunting since, in their reverence for the past, they guaranteed that its treasures could survive into our own time.

Roman manuscripts fared somewhat better than Greek, partly because Greece was distant and partly because classical Latin was more easily recovered than Greek. In the middle of the 14th century, both Petrarch and Boccaccio undertook to study Greek but from poor teachers. Not until the Byzantine scholar, Chrysolaurus, was inveigled to Florence in 1394 to teach Greek to anyone who would learn did a full knowledge reach the West. Then the Renaissance was able to enter the second temple of antiquity and to pay Greece its deserved homage. The fresh renderings of the Bible, already mentioned, utilized these new, more sophisticated, linguistic skills. At this point the Renaissance made its crucial contribution to the Reformation: for Luther repeatedly stressed that his grasp of the principle of "justification by faith" was prompted, aided, and sustained by linguistic insight.

Facility with Greek, combined with salvaged manuscripts from the East, meant the recovery of scriptural accuracy, poetry, drama, history, science, and geometry—Leonardo knew Euclid by heart —and of philosophy crowned by Plato and Aristotle. Both Plato and Aristotle had long been available in Europe; Plato by way of neo-Platonists and Aristotle by way of the Averroists. Now Plato could be studied in the original and Aristotle could be read unvarnished by Christian overlays. Padua became the chief of a number of universities with a heavy Aristotelian leaning, and Cosimo de Medici founded a Platonic academy in Florence in 1439. It nurtured devotees, like Ficino (1433-1499), who affirmed that Plato and Christianity were really compatible, and Giovanni Pico, Count of Mirandola (1463-1494), who was the most eclectic humanist of all.

Contact with the original sources in the original language encouraged a few advanced thinkers to revolutionize the philosophy of ethics. A number of pure Aristotelians disdained the pseudo-Aristotelianism of the scholastics. One of this group, Pietro

Pomponazzi (1462-1525) denied the immortality of the soul to show how much more virtuous life would be if it were lived for its own sake instead of for the hope of eternal reward. His view represented an extreme school, but moderate and even orthodox opinions moved in the same direction. There had long been a semi-Pelagian stream in Catholicism, allowing man some capacity and merit for good behavior; now the scope of man's ethical capability became greatly enlarged. Giovanni Pico, like Ficino, was a neo-Platonist and a devout Christian who, in the celebrated "Oration," ignored the cooperation of Christ and the sacraments in the process of moral improvement. "On the Dignity of Man" was added to the title later. Man was a creation of infinite variety and capacity. He could abase himself to the level of a brute or raise himself to the level of an angel, with the special help of philosophy. As Alberti, the architect, philosopher, and scientist observed, "Man can make whatever he will of himself."

Doctrines of this sort glorified individual human freedom and abandoned spiritual discipline. By asserting them, the more radical humanists were reviving a pagan philosophy of ethics that had been largely dormant since the Greeks. Man alone, and not God and grace, was the source of moral energy. In this aspect humanism stood in sharpest contrast to the Reformation. Luther was to have his most violent quarrel with Erasmus on the subject, though Erasmus was thoroughly moderate. The more radical philosophers were categorically rejecting the medieval past. Although St. Thomas said that grace had need of nature and reason, he firmly believed that grace was indispensible to the process of moral endeavor. The new Aristotelians, the neo-Platonists (absorbed by the phenomena of nature as a reflection of truth), Machiavelli, and the secular historians, were all unshackling the spirit of man from metaphysical trappings.

Religious trammels were not easily to be shed: Machiavelli and Pompanazzi were unusual. Such a luminary as the Frenchman, Jean Bodin (1529-1596), embedded some inconsistencies in his political theory because he could not discard all of the assumptions of the past. In the preamble to his great work on discovering universal law in history, he wrote, "Let us for a moment abandon the divine to the theologian, the natural to the philosophers, while we concentrate long and intently on human actions and the rules governing them." Bodin had moved a long way toward a naturalistic interpretation of history, law, and politics. But, having stressed the inalienable and indivisible nature of sovereignty, he limited it by divinely instituted natural laws—the law, for example, sustaining the right of private property. Eminent rationalist as he was, large-minded and tolerant as he was, he had no doubt whatsoever about the reality of witchcraft. In this, he shared the virulent bigotry of his contemporaries. The tendency, which was recovered in the Renaissance, to discover laws and explanations within self-contained areas without recourse to divine causation must be viewed as a tendency only, a rivulet that would broaden and swell in the course of time. Since then, science and technology, statecraft and politics have become increasingly divorced from divine concerns and from ethics. Their separation from morality may be the gravest legacy of the Renaissance.

### THE BEGINNINGS OF SCIENCE

Both the naturalism of Aristotle and the idealism of Plato fed streams of scientific thought during later 15th and early 16th centuries. One should add that contact with Pythagoras revived number-mysticism, and that the classical legacy fostered many superstitions. If the most dramatic achievements of science awaited the 17th century, the spade-work for that growth was done in the Renaissance era. A technology had developed that made sophisticated observation possible. The telescope, which Galileo "invented" in 1609, was simply an improvement on earlier attempts. The telescope is a suggestive example, because it was the culmination of a long history of interest in lenses and optics that began with Grosseteste and Roger Bacon. As important as technology was the fresh absorption of the Renaissance with old problems. Experimentation (in the best Aristotelian tradition) and observation (after the recent fashion of artists) caused Vesalius to correct 200 errors of Galen in his study of human anatomy (1543).

Plato's celebrated analogy of God and the sun in the allegory of the cave contributed both to the artists' and to the mathematicians' fascination with light and space. The problem of perspective became both an artistic and scientific one, and no distinction existed between these pursuits. If Leonardo da Vinci was outstanding in both fields—and in engineering, hydraulics, and hydrostatics as well—there were many like him. Around 1400 the architect, Brunelleschi (1377-1446), constructed an optical instrument—a camera obscura—for the express purpose of studying perspective scientifically, and that meant mathematically, yet he achieved this device through experimentation.

After this, there was a slow shift of attention from the substance of objects to their function and form. Also there was a shift from a mechanical to an abstract mathematical approach to natural problems. Both of these tendencies were the harbingers of the great scientific revolution that followed. Copernicus' (1473-1543) famous heliocentric view of the universe, in opposition to the old Ptolemaic geocentric system, was a better (more economical) perspective construction. "Where," he asked in neo-Platonic language, "should the lamp of the Universe be rightly placed except at the center?" These men were both visionaries and scientists. Using Tycho Brahe's (1546-1601) minute observations of the heavens, Kepler (1571-1630) was able to correct some of Copernicus' inaccuracies. He showed that the earth's orbit is elliptical rather than circular and laid down laws governing its movement. We shall refer to this subject again in the last chapter. His hypotheses conformed to observation rather than to a neat geometrical pattern. But Kepler, too, was something of a mystic. Many of his hypotheses were wildly erroneous. Since he was preoccupied with space, he gave thought to optical problems such as the refraction of light: he had a sensible theory of vision. Hand in hand, technology, science, art, philosophy and, above all, curiosity and imagination paved the way for Galileo, Descartes, and Newton.

Until the arrival of photography and, more recently, of plastic models, the descriptive sciences such as botany, biology, and anatomy were the direct beneficiaries of art. Even today the illustrations in anatomy and botany books are hand-drawn. Artists, earlier than physicians or surgeons, practiced dissection to satisfy their curiosity about the human form.

### ART AND ARCHITECTURE

The artists' quest for physical naturalism in painting and sculpture was studded with mistakes until the sixteenth century; and,

Donatello, *Atys-amorino* (Brogi-Art Reference Bureau, Bargello, Florence).
Donatello, *Mary Magdalen* (Brogi-Art Reference Bureau, Ballestero, Florence).

by then, the strictly naturalistic movement had run its course. Often it is in "mistakes" that one can find an artist's intentions most surely displayed. Donatello (about 1386-1466) gave a chubby little child an overmuscular torso in *Atys-amorino* (Time as a Playful Child Throwing Dice) because he could not resist the urge to get beneath the subcutaneous fat to the structure beneath. His realism went beyond mere accurate reporting: it is fired with intense pathos in his *Mary Magdalen,* and with sublime peace in his *Virgin and Child.*

Donatello, *Virgin and Child* (Victoria and Albert Museum).

Neither realism nor expressiveness originated with Donatello, though he brought these trends to their climax. Nor was realism peculiarly Italian. It belonged to an international style. Yet the realism of the North was more social than anatomical. Classical models were less influential there, and painting rather than sculpture dictated the norms of style. Moreover, the prestige of Jan van Eyck (1385?-1441), who perfected oil painting (mixing oil with pigment), was sufficient to mold subsequent style for a century. *The Crucifixion* (painted by van Eyck and/or his brother,

Jan and/or Hubert van Eyck, *The Crucifixion* (The Metropolitan Museum of Art, Fletcher Fund, 1933).
Jan van Eyck, *Adam and Eve* (Bruckmann-Art Reference Bureau, Church of St. Bravo, Ghent).

Hubert) depicts the scene as it probably was—something of a gala occasion. His nudes (*Adam and Eve*) lack the muscular exactness of Italian work, but they are to be considered more realistic on that account. After van Eyck, Netherlandish art, in particular, and Northern art, in general, never lost its homely touch. Social realism became stronger until it passed sometimes beyond social comment to sermons on the predicament of man. The meticulous

Albrecht Dürer, *Melancholia* (Fogg Art Museum, Harvard University).

German, Dürer (1471-1528), who specialized in realistic engrav-
ings and woodcuts, portrayed his own doubts about the ultimate
meaning of art and of human endeavors in *Melancholia*. Here, a
bluestocking sits in idleness while craftsmen toil and the symbols
of the professions lie neglected and abandoned around about her;
and a pair of dividers—a comment perhaps in the geometric
artistry of Italy—lies unnoticed beneath her finger; an hourglass
measures the march of time above her, the bell tolls a knell, the
comet is a portend of disaster. Only the child, in her innocence,
escapes despondency. Dürer, after his conversion to Lutheranism,
devoted all of his talent and realism to works of "strangely im-
passioned austerity." Meanwhile the Netherlander, Bosch (about
1450-1516?), ventured beyond realism into what might be

Hieronymus Bosch, *Christ before Pilate* (The Art Museum, Princeton University).

called religious surrealism. In his *Christ before Pilate* the expressions on the faces have gone beyond human expression to gargoylesque caricature.

It is normal to trace expressionism back to the Italian Masaccio (1401-1428), but there were signs of it earlier. In the 13th and early 14th centuries, Nicola Pisano and his son, Giovanni, mark an early stage in the transition from medieval craftsman to self-conscious modern artist. Father and son carved magnificent pulpits: Nicola at Siena (*Duomo,* 1265-1268) and Giovanni at Pisa (*Duomo,* 1302-1310). Crowded into Giovanni's carving in scenes such as the crucifixion, are agony, pain, resignation, sorrow, and malevolence. Masaccio was reaching back to this rich style in his *Expulsion of Adam and Eve.* In both cases there is penetrating psychological insight into a fateful episode in man's spiritual history. Masaccio's Adam holds his head in his hands in deep remorse, while Eve, whose face we see, is racked by unutterable shame and despair. The idea of investing a great moment of

Giovanni Pisano, Pulpit in the Duomo, Pisa (Anderson-Art Reference Bureau).

An early fourteenth century *Pieta*, showing the late medieval idea of heightening the emotion of a biblical moment (Marburg-Art Reference Bureau, Provincial Museum, Bonn).

Masaccio, *Expulsion of Adam and Eve* (Taurgo Slides).

Christian history with profound emotion was late medieval, and the Renaissance merely applied it with a more telling technique.

Late medieval pathos was perhaps easier to realize in sculpture than in painting, since sculpture was three-dimensional when painting had not yet mastered the portrayal of depth and space. With Giotto, there is a beginning of naturalism still couched in formality, and there is the suggestion of a sense of space in his segmented sky in *The Lamentation*. Giotto (1266-1337), born near Florence, was his father's shepherd. As a boy his delight in nature impelled him to capture it on rock or sand or wherever he could. Discovered by another artist, he was taken into the artist's workshop and, with guidance, became the first to attempt

Giotto, *The Lamentation* (Alinari-Art Reference Bureau, Chapel of Scrovegni all'Arena, Padua).

Taddeo Gaddi, *The Presentation of the Virgin* (Alinari-Art Reference Bureau, Church of Santa Croce, Florence).

Two versions of Venus with the Sea Goose from one of Ovid's works: the earlier one (*left*, about 1380) from the Bibliothèque Nationale shows the flat medieval background, the later one (*right*, about 1480) shows the movement to deep landscape (Art Reference Bureau, The Royal Library, Copenhagen).

honest likeness and naturalism in his figures and to grapple with problems of perspective. Renaissance art may be said to begin here.

The struggle of the artists to master perspective resulted in a series of heroic, if luckless, attempts. Taddeo Gaddi's *Presentation of the Virgin* (1338) is such a piece. The vast chasm between 14th- and 15th-century ability to portray depth on a flat surface can be shown by a commonplace illustration from two editions of the same book a century apart. In the later illustration the beauties follow Eyck's ideal rather than the manly and sometimes Amazonian Italian concept of womanhood. Perhaps there was regional variation in physique. Cupid has changed from a crowned angel into a lecherous courtier, the attendants are wholly disrobed, and there is greater facility in the drawing of figures and the water surface but, most obvious and most important, the flat medieval background has become a deep, distant landscape. Space-denying art had given way to space-affirming art.

It seems clear that perspective was finally conquered in the

Filippo Brunelleschi, *Sacrifice of Isaac* (Alinari-Art Reference Bureau, Museo Nazionale, Florence).

late 14th century. Although Brunelleschi had invented the perspective instrument (the camera obscura) around 1400, there were men—or one, at least—whose control of depth was more confident than his. In 1401 Brunelleschi's bronze panel of the *Sacrifice of Isaac,* submitted to a competition for the contract to build doors for the Baptistry in Florence, was defeated by a panel of Ghiberti's (1378-1455). Both panels exist, and no one has ever thought that the original verdict was wrong. Ghiberti's conception was more compact. His young Isaac is a work of breath-taking

Lorenzo Ghiberti, *Sacrifice of Isaac* (Alinari-Art Reference Bureau, Museo Nazionale, Florence).

beauty, closely modeled on a classical torso that he had in his possession. Depth was achieved by overlapping the figures in the foreground, and placing them over rockery behind. To complete the effect, the shoulders of both Abraham and Isaac slant into the panel itself. By comparison, Brunelleschi's attempt seems stilted. After losing the competition, and the contract worth well over two million dollars in modern currency, Brunelleschi gave up sculpturing in disgust and made himself the most influential architect of the Renaissance.

Brunelleschi's dome on the Cathedral in Florence (Alinari-Art Reference Bureau).

He did not skimp any effort to accomplish this. He measured Roman ruins, pondered the hypothesized, and came to the conclusion that the classical principle of harmony consisted in having a module (a unit of measure) that could be divided into every important dimension. Whether this mathematical principle of ratio and proportion is better than any other, or better than no principle at all, is an open question. In any event, Brunelleschi revived the style of early Christian basilicas (which he took to be classical) by balancing blocks of space and by using his principle of proportion throughout. His credentials as an architect were confirmed when he won the competition, staged by the equivalent of a Public Works Committee, for a design for a dome to complete the crossing of the Cathedral in Florence. It must be said that the organizers of the competition showed great daring. They called for a dome 150 feet in diameter, larger than the dome of *Hagia Sophia,* when nobody in the Western world knew how to build one. No dome had been built since the 10th century, when St. Sophia's dome had last collapsed. Undaunted, Brunelleschi designed a high dome, raised on a drum (cylinder) and ringed with chains under tension to contain the thrust. Domes were

Leonardo da Vinci, *Adoration of the Magi;* uses geometrical constructions (Alinari-Art Reference Bureau, Uffizi, Florence).

built the same way thereafter, until the advent of ferro-concrete.

Brunelleschi exemplified the arrogant freedom of Renaissance genius. Not only did he provide a definitive solution to the architectural (or engineering) problem, but he devised his own original methods of construction and cowed the guild workers who resented his independence.

The dome is really a synthesis of philosophy and architecture in the service of science and religion. Brunelleschi's friend and adviser, the scientist, Toscanelli, had him place a perforated bronze plate in such a position on top of the dome that a shaft of light fell on a graduated cement strip below. It was a dial device, which enabled Toscanelli to measure the angle of the plane of the sun's apparent orbit around the earth with remark-

Leonardo da Vinci, *Mona Lisa* (Art Reference Bureau, Louvre, Paris).

Raphael, *The Dispute* (Vatican Museum).

able accuracy. In other words, the Cathedral's dome was partly an observatory. It was also a religious experience. For the dome rises in segments whose lines slowly converge to meet, so it seems, somewhere in infinity. It was an allegory of philosophical contemplation of the Infinite Being, carrying the heart, with the eye, to the heavens.

With a similar intent, Renaissance painters, after Brunelleschi, used geometric constructions and perspective skill for contemplative and religious purposes. The vanishing point of Leonardo da Vinci's *Adoration of the Magi* leads to infinity. By this time, uniform space had become the common property of artists and it remained typical of European art until the 20th century. There, too, is pathos worthy of Masaccio and a blurring of forms whose shapes are merely suggested in the shadows. This clever manipulation of light and shade is called chiaroscuro—and there is no architectural equivalent for it. In *Mona Lisa* there are two distinct horizons, to heighten the mystery of the face. All this shows that by the high Renaissance the artist's use of dimensions had become highly self-conscious, complex, and articulate. Whereas, in the *Adoration,* Leonardo used triangles to give unity to his groupings, Raphael (1483-1520), in *The Dispute,* used different geometric constructions, noticeably the semicircle after the semidomes common in architecture. In this work Raphael placed the wafer, held in the monstrance, precisely on the vanishing point. So everything converged there. By this device Raphael could subtly announce his faith in the doctrine of transubstantiation. To him, there was no dispute, and his art was a testimony to his orthodox theology.

It is a useful corrective, with respect to the view that the Renaissance was pagan, to realize that many of its finest works contained theological lessons, that Michelangelo's most classical sculpture was a David, and not an Apollo. On the other hand, it is true that Renaissance art and architecture were more man-centered than formally symbolic. Symbolism and allegory persisted throughout the Renaissance but with attributes portrayed in realistic fashion. There was a tide of anthropocentrism sweeping in, and work like Bosch's, which stood against it, seems strange and puzzling in the context.

Whereas Gothic style, in church building, had strived for ethe-

Ca d'Oro in Venice, which utilizes the idea of "functional voids" (Alinari-Art Reference Bureau).

Brunelleschi's Foundling Hospital in Florence (Alinari-Art Reference Bureau).

Antonio Pollaiuolo, *The Battle of Ten Naked Men* (The Metropolitan Museum of Art, Purchase 1917, Joseph Pulitzer Bequest).

real space, the Renaissance juxtaposed space and solidity (the spaces are known as functional voids) to give a feeling of well-being on earth. In some Venetian palaces and in Brunelleschi's Foundling Hospital in Florence, space shapes were used to lend elegance, grace, and repose to the whole. The void became an integral component of order and harmony.

Artists, like Antonio Pollaiuolo (about 1430-1498), were as much concerned with shapes of their interstices as with the figures. In his engraving, *The Battle of Ten Naked Men,* there is—as in Donatello—a fixation on anatomy. Pollaiuolo may have been the first to dissect bodies for insight into their structure. But also the battle is an elaborate and angular pictorial design. By means of curves and angles of tension, and by means of his swirling background, he managed to heighten the motion and ferocity of the fighting bodies.

Again and again the Renaissance greets us with its interpenetration of disciplines and its striking cross-fertilizations between what, to us, are separate fields of endeavor. Alberti (1404-1472) is another example—a painter, sculptor, and architect but, above all, a philosopher whose aesthetic theories have dominated art

Leone Battista Alberti, Basilica of San Andrea in Mantua (Alinari-Art Reference Bureau).

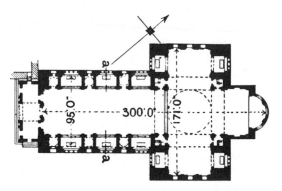

Plan of San Andrea in Mantua (From *A History of Architecture* by Sir Banister Fletcher, courtesy of Athlone Press, London).

Alberti, Church of San Francesco in Rimini (Alinari-Art Reference Bureau).

and art criticism from the middle of the 15th to the 19th century. Beauty, for him, was an absolute abstract reality, existing independently of taste or caprice.

Not surprisingly he drew heavily on current practice, despite his idealism, when he tried to implement his theories, but he added his own distinctive notions to contemporary stock. He simplified Brunelleschi's basic basilican pattern in his design for the church of San Andrea in Mantua. Also he made the facade and interior much grander, heavier, and perhaps less elegant. A comparison of Alberti's remodeling of the church of San Francesco in Rimini with Brunelleschi's Foundling Hospital shows sharply the gravity and stolidity of the church. All of Alberti's proportions were heavier and all of his solids were more obvious. In the design for San Andrea, Alberti used what is technically known as colossal order in the facade. That is, he ran his pilasters onward and upward through two horizontal divisions. Thus the four great verticals lend the facade a grandeur that four columns, broken by horizontals, could never do.

Sandro Botticelli, *The Birth of Venus* (Alinari-Art Reference Bureau, Uffizi, Florence).

Alberti's aesthetic theory was bolstered by the popularity of the Platonism that was spreading from the Florentine Academy in the late 15th century. Renaissance Platonism reinstated the medieval virtue of contemplation, but with this difference: laymen practiced it in thought and action rather than monks by prayer and fasting. Platonic ideals were considered parts of God himself. Therefore the contemplation of ideals like beauty or love was invested with a certain religious significance.

Botticelli (1444/5-1510) was the embodiment of artistic Platonism: his *Birth of Venus,* with its watery hues and airy spaciousness, was a hymn to beauty and love. Venus, gently wind-blown and floating on a cockle shell, is welcomed to shore by Spring holding a garlanded gown. The face of Venus is quiet and sad, and her contemplative mood fills the canvas. And, in architecture, Raphael's dome on *Sant' Eglio degli Orifici* suggests the Platonic cosmos itself. By separating the drum from the supports (pendentives) and then the dome from the drum, Raphael was allegorizing the Platonic world system in which all things are arranged in categories, the higher being the better and more beautiful, and

Raphael, Dome of Sant Eglio degli Orifici (Gabinetto Fotografico Nazionale-Art Reference Bureau).

Raphael, *Portrait of Pope Leo X with His Nephews* (Alinari-Art Reference Bureau, Galleria Palatina).

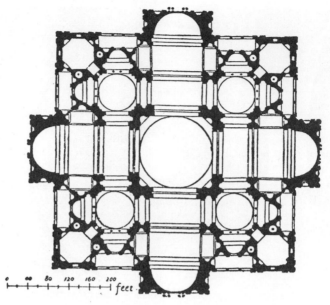

Donato Bramante, Plan for Saint Peter's in Rome, 1506 (From *An Outline of European Architecture* by Nikolaus Pevsner, used with permission of Penguin Books, Ltd.)

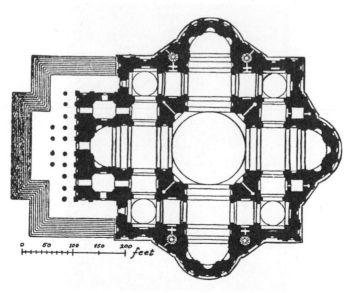

Michelangelo, Plan for Saint Peter's in Rome, 1546 (From *An Outline of European Architecture* by Nikolaus Pevsner, used with permission of Penguin Books, Ltd.)

Andrea Palladio, Villa Rotonda in Vicenza (Alinari-Art Reference Bureau).

closer to the nature of the Divine. Vasari called him a "mortal god." Yet he was not all pure spirit and undiluted light. His portraits were supremely realistic, and he was the quickest artist to take advantage of the new possibilities of the printing press by selling prints of his own paintings for profit.

Alberti's architectural style was closely studied by Bramante and Michelangelo. It was Alberti's idea to abandon the extended nave of the basilica and to develop a "central church" that both Bramante and Michelangelo followed in their plans for Saint Peter's. After the Council of Trent the old style was reinstated. St. Peter's nave was then extended, and the original conception was ruined. Michelangelo's architectural style was grand and ornate, so it is often said that the simpler Palladio (1508-1580) was more of a classicist, though he was born later. He published measured drawings of ancient buildings, with his own instructions for details of construction. These were widely translated and, in time, were circulated as far afield as the American frontier. His *Villa Rotonda* in Vincenza was somewhat like the central church plan in that the central chamber was domed. But is was surrounded by rectangular rooms, and every face was

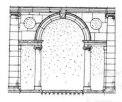

The Palladian window is based on this portico design from Palladio's *Four Books of Architecture,* Bk III, plate XIX, (London 1738). Very often a panelled or glass-paned door or pair of doors is centered under a fanlight window, flanked by panels of rectangular window-panes. Adapted from *A History of Architecture* by Sir Banister Fletcher, courtesy of Athlone Press, London.

graced, like the Pantheon, with columns and he added impressive staircases. It was widely imitated, but even more popular was his pleasing design for a window (or doorway). A round-capped opening is flanked by two lower and flat-headed openings. Pure forms of it, or variations, must number a million in the Western World. It is still called the Palladian Window.

Palladio's Villa Rotonda is monumental, but Alberti's grand manner reached its zenith with Michelangelo. In stone, in fresco and on canvas his figures are heroes and demigods. Adam in *The Creation of Adam,* on the roof of the Sistine Chapel, is a dynamo of controlled power languidly at rest. His *Captive Slaves* writhe in their stone. The hesitant steps of Giotto in the direction of tactile reality and sense of movement culminate with Michelangelo whose prestige in the Western world was rivaled only by Raphael.

Michelangelo personified the "cult of genius." From Brunelleschi's time the independence and authority of the artist was increasingly recognized. Alberti, unlike Brunelleschi, did not have to supervise his buildings; he merely drafted the plans. Patrons became tolerant of artistic temperament, for as Cosimo de Medici remarked of Fra Lippo Lippi, "One must treat these people of extraordinary genius as if they were celestial spirits, and not like beasts of burden." The material rewards of excellence were immense, and a talented artist could amass a considerable fortune. The greatest became "stars" whose art had been the avenue of rapid social advancement. Often of petty bourgeois or lower social origin, they were now accepted on terms of equality by the highest nobility. Late Renaissance grandiosity may reflect this "arrival" of the artist, and it may also display the increasing affluence and power of their upper-class patrons.

The revival of a sumptuous courtly style in portraiture and of medieval pageant scenes in modern idiom is some evidence of the

Michelangelo, *The Creation of Adam* (Alinari-Art Reference Bureau, the Sistine Chapel).

Michelangelo, *Captive Slave* (Alinari-Art Reference Bureau, Galleria Antica e Moderna, Florence).

Hans Holbein, *Henry VIII*, Alinari-Art Reference Bureau, Galleria Corsini, Rome).

fame and affluence of these patrons. Holbein's *Henry VIII* glorifies regal power and ruthless majesty. Perugino's (about 1450-1523) *The Delivery of the Keys*, with Alberti's ideal church, and Arches of Constantine in the background, is an early example of pageant style that retains some gravity and dignity suitable to the occasion. The Venetian School later slaked their insatiable appetites for color on similar themes. Veronese's (1528-1588) *Marriage at Cana* is a rich and gaudy gathering.

Pietro Perugino, *The Delivery of the Keys* (Vatican Museum).

Paolo Veronese, *Marriage at Cana* (Alinari-Art Reference Bureau, Louvre, Paris).

Tintoretto, *The Presentation of the Virgin* (Alinari-Art Reference Bureau, dell'Orte, Venice).

Tintoretto, *The Last Supper* (Alinari-Art Reference Bureau, Church of St. Giorgio Maggiore, Venice).

The Venetians developed a special ability to dramatize an event with shafts of luminous light piercing deep shadow. Tintoretto (1518-1594) made use of the light in his *Presentation of the Virgin* and also in *The Last Supper*, presented as something of a feast, in contrast to the usually restrained treatments of the theme. The Venetians indulged in the lush and plush, as Giorgione's (1477/8-1510) *Sleeping Venus* shows when contrasted to Botticelli's *Birth of Venus*. Titian (1490-1576) carried on the tradition of nudes fleshier than naturalistic, but he was more of an idealist than Giorgione. In his *Bacchanale* there is no movement in the bodies, no passionate frenzy: instead there is a mild revel or romp that he could build into a canvas of placid and resonant colors. The passivity—even in his most dramtic work— suggests the placidity of Venice herself. Although Venice suffered in her mainland possessions, she was free from the successive foreign invasions that shook the mainland. No conqueror set foot in Venice until Napoleon Bonaparte. Isolated and serene in this island world, the Renaissance could continue in dignified repose. But elsewhere it was subject to violent disruption.

From Giotto to Michelangelo, Renaissance artists and architects had grappled with a series of specific problems (perspective, expression, form and space) and had mastered all of them brilliantly. Unlike classical art, which moved from idealism to realism, the opposite movement occurred. The early 15th-century concern with space led to a somewhat static and artificial style in the late 15th century. Then the simplicity, harmony, and monumentality of the early Michelangelo gave way to disintegration, seen in Leonardo's interest in flux and change; an ultra realism, that hardened into "mannerism"—the sculpturelike, distorted art of Michelangelo's middle period. Similarly, architecture traced regressive steps from Gothic style back to antiquity. But, of course, the idealism and classicism of the Renaissance were more complex and grander in conception and execution than the ancients had attempted. Renaissance art, after all, served an ampler and less simple society. The journey back had not brought back the past, but had hastened the dawning of new styles.

Giorgione, *Sleeping Venus* (Staatliche Kunstammlungen, Dresden).

Titian, *Bacchanale* (Museo del Prado, Madrid).

THE INVASIONS OF ITALY

By the end of the 15th century, Italy was a fruit ripe for the plucking. In contrast to the nation-states of the North and West, she was divided, vulnerable, wealthy, and worth more in prestige than florins. Italy brought disaster on herself, since it was Lodovico Sforza, the tyrant of Milan, who caused an invasion by issuing an open invitation to France for support. Pietro de Medici of Florence had disrupted the balance of power, or concert, of Italy by acknowledging the claims of Naples in Milan. Hitherto these three states had kept a tenuous alliance, and the peace of Italy depended on it. When the alliance was discarded the subsequent collapse of equilibrium tantalized outside powers. France and Spain had just entered on the shining patrimony of internal unity and peace, and were now free to dabble in Italian politics. It may well be that expansive drives are an inseparable condition of national status, which ineluctable possibility may underlie the struggle for mastery of Europe that has been waging ever since.

Charles VIII entered Italy in 1494, hoping to reenact the exploits of Charlemagne, to conquer Naples and eventually, to wrest Constantinople from the Turks. The North allowed him free passage; Florence prepared to fight but, at the first sight of an encounter, Pietro de Medici capitulated. The Florentines subsequently drove Pietro and his brood into exile for his cowardice. Rome opened its gates without invitation and the slaughter of the inhabitants of two towns on the Neopolitan border brought about the surrender of Naples. After months of jousting and tournaments. Charles returned home and no one knows what became of his designs.

As the ferocity of the French, in their brief skirmishes, had terrified Italy, so had the ease of conquest inflamed French ambition. Charles' successor, Louis XII, claimed succession to Milan through the female line of the Visconti family and entered the city to claim his inheritance in 1499. He defeated Milan and pressed on to Naples, only to fall out with Spain and leave in 1502. Back in Milan, Louis joined a League of Cambrai with the Pope and with Maximilian Hapsburg of Austria for the purpose of stripping Venice of her mainland possessions. The Pope proved a fickle ally. He feared the French and, when he had what he wanted, turned against Louis and formed a Holy League to drive him out of the country. With the help of the Spanish he succeeded, though not before the French won the bloody battle of Ravenna. The tyrannical Sforzas were returned to Milan and the Medicis to Florence. The Medici family had dissipated their wealth in exile and had forgotten their republican sympathies. Machiavelli was tortured at this time because of imprudent devotion to the republic, but he hastened to rectify his mistake. He retired to write his *The Prince* and attached a fawning dedication to Lorenzo de Medici in the hope of favor.

France returned to Milan in 1515, and all the Pope could think to do was enlist the support of the Emperor. In 1519 Maximilian I was succeeded by Charles V, hereditary ruler of Spain, Burgundy, and heir to Hapsburg territories as well. But Spanish and German troops proved as insupportable as French. The Pope indulged in a series of shifting alliances and unsuccessful military maneuvers, only to witness the sacking of Rome. Not all of the Pope's diplomatic dodging could save Rome from a despoilation more terrible than that of the Goths and of the Vandals. Pillage, rapine, murder, and extortion reigned from 1527 to 1528. Finally, Charles V made peace with France and with the papacy, although he had no internal need to do so—he had not been defeated—but wider European concerns diverted his attention. The Reformation had divided Germany, and the Turks were camping under the walls of Vienna.

Florence lost its republican constitution once and for all in 1530. Siena presently fell to Florence. Of the little republics, Genoa and Lucca enjoyed the name but not the reality of liberty. The rest made themselves dutiful fiefs of the empire; so that, of all the major states, Venice alone remained in undisturbed possession of its republicanism.

A swift twilight had fallen on the Italian states' independence. The devastations and victories of the invading armies subdued the elated tone of the Italian Renaissance. Gucciardini and

Leonardo da Vinci, *The Deluge;* (The Royal Library, Windsor Castle).

Machiavelli mark the change of mood. Leonardo da Vinci's sketches of battles and floods are alive with turbulence. Michelangelo's *Last Judgment* throbs with violence, despair and disarray. Classical harmony was dissolving.

Yet vitality continued. The waters of the Renaissance mingled with those of the Reformation in the North. The best of Italian literature and music was yet to come. Catholic theology was to be recast near Italian soil by Italian clergy. Italy was yet to give Galileo to science. Her commerce would be overshadowed, but its decline was not absolute, only relative. Epochs blend into one another; it is the historians who separate them.

Michelangelo, *The Last Judgment* (Anderson-Art Reference Bureau, the Sistine Chapel).

# 5

# The Transformation of
# Europe on the Eve
# of the Reformation

In the latter half of the 15th century Europe underwent changes that belong as much, or more, to the Reformation as to the Renaissance. Some of the changes were dramatic breakthroughs—the invention of printing, the use of gunpowder in warfare, the discovery of the new world. Others were not instant but, nonetheless, were startling. Of these changes a price rise, accompanying the recovery of European trade, increased by leaps and bounds in and throughout the 16th century. At the same time there was a radical upswing in population. It has been believed that the vitality of Italian thought declined as wealth increased. More properly the loss of vitality should be linked to the loss of political independence, for in England the Renaissance flowered late, beside growing wealth and alongside a national self-consciousness that was one of the results of the French victory in the Hundred Years War.

Despite such nascent patriotism, the values of the humanists managed to encompass the educated European world without the support of a powerful institution. Humanism, in its broadest sense, was an international idiom. Humanists' success resulted from the availability of the printing press, of course, but while they profited from the wider diffusion and the greater popularity of their interests, printing in no way altered the quality of their appeal. However, this can be said of the impact of printing on the Reformation. The Reformation was not to be an aristocratic or élitist movement.

Theologians faced Europe with the knowledge that the watchwords which they thundered would reach literate people whereever books and pamphlets could penetrate. Very shortly after it began, the Reformation became a mass movement, involving all classes down to the scarcely literate. This was the result of printing. Like children born with silver spoons in their mouths, Reformation theologians found that the means of mass dissemination was both an advantage and an embarrassment.

PRINTING

A discussion of printing, as though it were an entirely novel thing, refers strictly to the invention of movable metal type. Between 1440 and 1450, John Gutenberg perfected the idea in Mainz and entered a partnership. Of course, as with most inventions, the ingredients were available: there was paper; artist's oil paint could be easily modified for a suitable ink; imprints were used in the textile trade, and even separate letter stamps were used in foundries to identify metal wares. Books already were being printed by the use of wooden blocks; and block books continued to compete with type-formed books for a period; indeed, for work that required no revisions, block prints were better. Movable type vastly increased the range and flexibility of production, and cheapened its cost, and woodcuts continued to be set in type for illustrations.

Within two decades, printers had carried their skills from Mainz to every corner of Europe. Latin was the original style though by 1465 Greek was in use, then vernacular types were cut, and even such difficult technical problems as geometry diagrams and music were being mastered.

Before 1470 a Frenchman, Nicholas Jensen, developed a readable, clean, well-spaced type called Roman, and he cut a clear Gothic and a splendid Greek font. To this day his letter designs are standards of beauty and balance in printing. The famous

PETRI BEMBI DE AETNA AD
ANGELVM CHABRIELEM
LIBER.

Factum a nobis pueris est, et quidem se-
dulo Angele; quod meminisse te certo
scio;ut fructus studiorum nostrorum,
quos ferebat illa aetas nó tam maturos, q̄
uberes,semper tibi aliquos promeremus:
nam siue dolebas aliquid,siue gaudebas;
quae duo sunt tenerorum animorum ma
xime propriae affectiones; continuo ha-
bebas aliquid a me,quod legeres,uel gra-
tulationis,uel consolationis;imbecillum
tu quidem illud,et tenue; sicuti nascentia
omnia,et incipientia;sed tamen quod es-
set satis amplum futurum argumentum
amoris summi erga te mei. Verum po-
stea,q̄ annis crescentibus et studia,et iudi
cium increuere; nósq̄; totos tradidimus
graecis magistris erudiendos; remissiores
paulatim facti sumus ad scribendum, ac
iam etiam minus quotidie audentiores.

A

LIB.III.

V t uidet ingenti saueuia templa reuelli
M ole,rapit gressus,er Caesaris a gmina rumpens,
A nte fores non dum reserata constitit aedis,
V squeadeo solus ferrum,mortemq̄; timere
A uri nescit amor, pereunt discrimine nullo
A missae leges,sed pars uilissima rerum
C erunitur mouisse opes,prohibenisq̄; rapina
V lchrem clara instituit uoce tribunus,
N on nisi per nostrum nobis percussa patebunt
T empla latus,nulla siq̄; fores nisi sanguine sacro
S parsas rapter opes,ceru uiolata potestas
I nuenit ista Deos, Crassiunisq̄; in bella securi
S aua tribunitiae uocerunt praelia dirae.
D etuge iam ferrum,neq̄; enim tibi turba uerenda est
S pectherix scelerum,deserta starus;in urbe.
N on feret e nostro sceleraius praemia miles,
S unt quos prosternas populi, quae moenia dones,
P acti ad exhaustae spolium non aegit egressus,
B ellum Caesar habes-his magnam uictor in iram
V ocibus accensus,uanam spem mortis honestae
C onripis,haud inquit ungulo se polluet isto
N ostra Metelle manus,dignum te Caesaris ira
N ullus honos facit .te uindice tuta relicta est
L ibertas;non usqueadeo permiscuit omnis
L ongus summa dies,ut non,si uox Metelli
S eruentur leges,malint a Caesare tolli-
D ixerat,er non dum foribus cedente tribuno
A crior ira subit, senos circumspicit enses
O blitus simulare togam,tum Cotta Metellum
C ompulit audaci nimium desistere coepto-

A trio of common styles: Roman (*top left*) and Italic (*top right*) from the
Aldine Press; Gothic (*bottom*) from the Gutenberg Bible (British Museum,
Art Reference Bureau; Henry E. Huntington Library and Art Gallery).

printer, Aldus Mantius, turned to Jensen's types when he set up his Aldine press in Venice in 1490. From this press there flowed the first editions of the classics to appear in handy pocket (or satchel) size. Formerly they had been unwieldy folios. His are the forerunners of modern paperback or pocket books. Aldus also developed an italic type that completed the trio of common styles: Roman, Gothic, and italic. It is some indication of the growth and spread of printing that the Aldine press was but one of a hundred printing offices in Venice at the time.

What did they publish? The Italians welcomed editions of the classics, while the Germans' output was more heavily religious. Overall, religious topics accounted for more than half of the works published before 1500. The Church Fathers, St. Thomas and other scholastic works, edifying religious tracts, editions of canon law and, above all, the Bible were most sought after. The Vulgate (Latin) Bible went through 133 editions in the 15th century, and it entered numerous vernacular printings in German, French, and Italian. There were fewer publications in Bohemian, Spanish, and Dutch, and none in English until the next century. Thomas à Kempis' *The Imitation of Christ* proved a best seller, and Savonarola's sermons were most popular.

If anything, public taste was old fashioned. In science, books of alchemy and witchcraft and recipes for miraculous herbal cures vied with Galen in medicine and Ptolemy in astronomy. Numerous medieval commentaries on Aristotle appeared alongside Pliny's *Natural History* and similar encyclopedic works from antiquity.

To their credit, presses in the early decades managed to issue a vast backlog of writing, dating back to Aesop's *Fables* and beyond. Contemporary work formed a slender proportion of the whole, and the fact that few authors were published in their own time suggests that the reading public was as busy, or busier, devouring the past as keeping up with the present.

EXPLORATION

One contemporary, however, did receive instant publication. *A Letter of Christopher Columbus Concerning the Newly Discovered Islands* was published as a leaflet in Barcelona in 1493.

Within a year, twelve editions appeared from Rome to Antwerp with translations and further editions to follow. Already, enthralling tales of travel and of the marvels of other worlds from men like Marco Polo enjoyed considerable vogue. Columbus' tale was not altogether free of falsehood, but it did more than cater to a taste prepared in advance. His journey established that Europe would extend its influence over the globe, would embroil the world in its continental struggles, and would dispense its technology, religion, and values to the nethermost regions. At one bound, Columbus had reopened the frontiers of Europe.

For all his vision, Columbus' dreams turned to dust. The unwavering faith he had placed in Toscanelli's calculations for the western route to China supported his feat, only to disappoint him in the end. He was a Genoese who had sailed in the Portuguese service and had mastered every advance then current in Mediterranean navigation—the compass, the astrolabe, the latest charts, and the stern-post rudder. Fired with a desire to do what others had guessed at, he nursed and touted the idea of sailing into the unknown for years before he finally gained support from Spain. His contract guaranteed him 10 percent of the returns from his discoveries.

After 10 weeks at sea, in October 1492, he landed in the Bahamas and was convinced that he had discovered islands just off the coast of Cathay. On his return he enjoyed a brief summer of glory; he was feted by the populace and the government named him Admiral of the Ocean and Viceroy of the Islands.

But, of course, Toscanelli's calculations had been wrong, and Columbus had traveled only halfway to his goal. All his later voyages (1494-1504) bore out this bitter truth. The islands yielded little gold, and a colony that he had planted in Haiti (Hispaniola) gave so much trouble that his reputation as an administrator was destroyed. He was sent back from his third voyage in fetters, to be released at home, but to be stripped of his titles. His contract was broken, so he spent his last days near poverty. He hoped that his rights would be renewed and, dreaming beyond the grave, disposed of vast sums in his will.

Even the continents whose Isthmus he discovered were named after another explorer, Amerigo Vespucci who sailed in 1497 and 1499. Amerigo claimed Brazil for Portugal and Cabot, a

Venetian, explored Nova Scotia for England. By 1497 it was beyond doubt that new continents had been discovered. Although Columbus came close to seeing the ocean that separated him from China, it was not until 1513 that Balboa gazed upon it from a peak near the gulf of Darien.

To this date Spain's spectacular explorations had brought her

Wood engraving from Columbus' letter of 1493. While this is not the Santa Maria, it is a typical explorer's vessel. As the engraving suggests, these ships were not large: the Santa Maria was 117 feet long and the two caravels which accompanied her on the voyage were only 50 feet long (New York Public Library).

scant reward, whereas little Portugal, whose feats were less impressive, was already reaping the harvest of overseas trade.

Portugal's methods contrasted sharply with those of Columbus. Columbus had ventured a breath-taking leap of imagination while the Portuguese sailors traversed the known over and over again before venturing any further. The courageous sailing into the sunset was not for them; they hugged the coast, feeling their way hesitantly and empirically.

Despite persistent encouragement from the third son of the King, Prince Henry the Navigator, the Portuguese sailors were, for a decade, too fearful to venture farther south than Cape Bojador (Northwest Africa); and, although Henry set up a school of navigation and equipped it with the latest charts and instruments, by the time of his death (1460) his protegés had not passed Sierra Leone—a mere 1000 miles—in 50 years. At least the lure of trade had begun to encourage others. In 1488, Diaz rounded the Cape of Good Hope because of the prospect it gave for reaching India. At this point, if the Crown had been less preoccupied with finding the coastal route to the East, Columbus may have been kept in Portuguese employ, and Portugal may have owned the world. As it was, the reward waited until 1497 when Vasco da Gama reached India.

Not without difficulty the Portuguese elbowed the Arab traders from their sphere of influence. Then they threw out a far-flung line of trading posts from Calicut, through Malacca to Macao, near Canton, in China itself. By 1520, the Genoese and Venetians, whose ties were with the Arabs, had been undercut, and the price of spices began to drop in spite of a general inflation. From this time the Mediterranean declined as the centerboard of commerce, and did not revive until the Suez Canal was cut in 1869. With the spice market saturated, slaves proved to be a more reliable staple but, since this was a trade whose bulk did not pass through Lisbon, Portugal never became a great commercial center.

Neither did Spain. Sizeable treasure arrived after 1502; it rose steadily after Cortes began his conquest of Montezuma's Aztec empire in Mexico in 1519. That same year Magellan left Seville, to die in an imbroglio in the Phillipines, but one of his three ships reached home three years later—the first ship ever to circumnavigate the world.

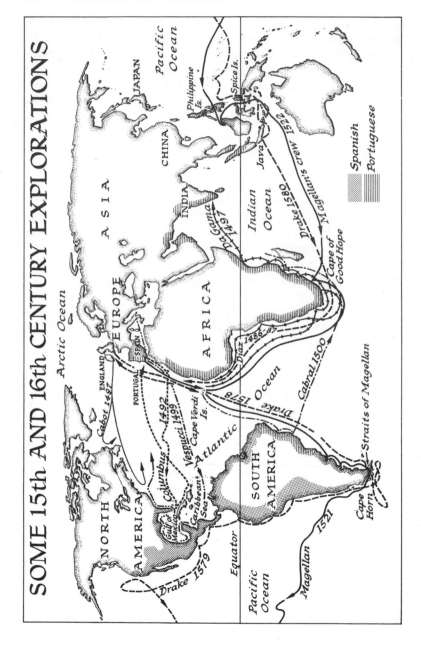

SOME 15th AND 16th CENTURY EXPLORATIONS

## TRADE AND COMMERCE

Spain had little industry and lacked the wares to export in return for the goods that the new world showered on her. Cadiz, the principal port, was in a poor geographical position to feed the distant European hinterlands, and the city was under severe restrictions from the Crown, who decreed who could trade there and on what terms. Thus, financiers operated through agents in Cadiz, preferring the freedom of Antwerp in the Netherlands.

Antwerp had long been famous for its fairs and its freedom. It had splendid access to the sea and to the interior, and deliberately cultivated its open and unrestricted market. Indeed, for the benefit of traders, in 1537 the city built the Bourse which became the model for those Exchanges at Amsterdam and London which would later succeed her in eminence. In the early 16th century, Antwerp was the hub of European commerce and the most cosmopolitan city in the world.

European commerce quickened on the gold and silver that began to reach Spain from Mexico and, after Pizarro's conquest of the Incas in the 1530's, on more silver from Peru. As fast as ingots came, Charles V spent them to supply his armies and to meet his creditors' high interest rates. Through the bankers it filtered down to the lowest levels, fomenting inflation as it went. Prices rose, credit became more abundant, and interest rates slowly fell. The Low Countries gradually replaced northern Italy as the commercial leader of Europe, but Italy still flourished. And, though less trade plied the route to Venice, Germany did not become a backwater overnight. Indeed, with the increased supply of bullion, German capitalists came into their own— Welsens, Haugs, Hochstetters, Imhofs and, greatest of them all, the Fuggers. The Fuggers never shifted their headquarters from Augsberg, though they drew their biggest profits from their Antwerp branch.

Reformation Germany, like all Europe, was beset by rising prices and also by an increase in the number of high bourgeoisie who were blamed for the spiral. Agricultural classes, from knights to peasants, found that the returns from their produce lagged behind the inflated prices of urban goods, and some ill-feeling was inevitable.

The dramatic upsurge of the 16th century had begun when gold dust began to reach Europe from Portuguese trading stations along the African coast and in the Congo basin. Slaves, ivory, ostrich plumes, parrots, and sugar filled their caravels, yet the exotic trade can be grossly exaggerated.

What mattered was the larger flow of staples: the exchange of the three main foodstuffs—cereals, fish, and wine—for industrial tools and textiles. Textiles were specialized. Italy still excelled in fine silks and satins, Germany in fustians, France and the Low Countries in linen, tapestries, and carpets, and England in wool and woolen cloth. Spain depended too heavily on raw wool production. The Baltic countries traded lumber and salted fish, Venice boasted delicate glassware, France and the Rhineland fine wines. Amsterdam led in shipbuilding. Eastern Europe and Sicily were the graneries that supplied the cereal-deficient areas of the Netherlands, northern Italy, Spain, and Portugal. At this time, rye was more important than wheat. All in all, Europe, on the eve of the Reformation, was more prosperous than it had ever been before.

POPULATION GROWTH

It was rapidly becoming more densely populated than ever before. Demographic histories testify that the 16th century saw a recovery of population from well below pre-Plague levels to well above them. The change from death surpluses to birth surpluses seems to have happened around the middle of the 15th century. Couples married younger and families grew larger. By the early 16th century, populations were still below pre-Plague figures, but in the remainder of the century a population revolution of staggering proportions was underway. In one of the best documented principalities of Germany the increase in population between 1500 and 1604 was 84 percent. Other areas appear to have had even greater increases. Detailed studies of parish registers in England (started in 1528) suggest a similar drastic trend. French figures are the same. All over Europe, in fact, a long upward wave had begun, which was not to subside until the middle of the 17th century. It would rise again in the 18th century. Why the baby boom should have started nobody quite knows, nor is it known why it stopped suddenly after our period. Why should thousands or millions of couples choose to enlarge or, later, to restrict the size of their families at roughly the same time? Although the relationship between culture, polities, and population growth (or decline) will long be debated, the relationship between growth within families and commercial expansion is a little better charted.

On the one hand, population growth expands markets, it increases mobility—"surplus" children would move to other villages or towns; and on the other hand, population growth makes the distress of bad harvests, famines, other disturbances, and deliberate depopulations more acute. That is, population growth encourages commercial growth but renders social problems more urgent and pressing. Maintenance of tillage, control of the poor, punishment of vagabonds, trading, manufacturing, and wage regulation become a matter of grave concern to governments. By the same token, social problems become a matter of unavoidable concern for reformers.

Population growth, it seems, has also an impact on rates of literacy. It was not the church schools nor the new secular foundations that carried the burden of mass education. Numerically, their influence was slight. In the dales and downs of the countryside, and in the villages, it was mothers of families who passed on literacy to their children. Reading and writing were family skills. At a certain point in the growth of a family a mother must have become too busy to teach all of her children. Except in London it seems that the less densely populated areas in the North and South of England remained at high levels of literacy, and the more densely populated Midlands and East-Anglia fell by comparison. Of course, it is only in a "conjugal" family unit (husband and wife only, without grandparents) that the burden of teaching falls on the mother. Throughout our period the percentage of "multigenerational" family units was low. This is a characteristic of the West—families set up separate economic units. In the East, married couples and their children normally lived with one set of parents or the other. It is an important social difference between East and West, but precisely where the line should be drawn in Europe is not quite clear. Nor, indeed, is it clear what inferences can safely be drawn from the pioneer work presently underway on literacy. The evidence is too flimsy to bear much weight. But perhaps an area of lowering literacy would be inclined to welcome Protestantism: it was a religion of the Word, with more oral instruction from the pulpits than Catholicism offered. And Protestantism was also an educational force since, in the main Protestant branches, children were intensively catechized. With Protestantism using the press and the pulpit, it is probably fair to assume that Europe's burgeoning population was becoming better informed on matters of general knowledge than previously.

### DIVIDED EUROPE

If Europeans were more knowledgeable, Europe (fortunately for the Reformers) was also more deeply divided than previously. If it had not been for the power struggle between Catholic Valois and Catholic Hapsburg the Reformation would have been nipped in the bud. Charles V earnestly desired it, but Francis I placed his political ambitions so far above religious principle that he encouraged the Protestant Cantons of Switzerland and the Lutheran princes in order to embarass the Emperor. He even allied himself with the infidel Turks.

By accident of inheritance, Charles V's lands encircled France and threatened to dominate the whole of the Continent. He claimed Burgundy, from Mary of Burgundy; he inherited Spain and its overseas Empire and Sicily and Naples from Ferdinand and Isabella; and he inherited the Hapsburg lands from Maximilian. It was far too much for one man to handle, and Charles chose to sacrifice the greatness of Spain for the will-o'-the-wisp prestige of the Empire. His own sense of justice defeated him, for he was pitted against a cunning and faithless opponent. Each victory was his; each time his moderate demands were met, only to be flouted at the first opportunity. After his sally to take the Imperial fief of Milan, for instance, Francis was captured in 1525. He agreed to waive his claim and pledged his good faith on the Gospels and before a wayside shrine. But, as soon as he reached France, he cried "Now I am King, I am King once more." He continued to press his claim for Milan on his own behalf and on behalf of his son (later Henry II) until mutual war-weariness brought the protracted and fitful war to a halt in the Treaty of Câteau Cambrésis in 1559.

Meanwhile the defeat that Charles had inflicted on the Lutheran princes in the Schmalkaldic League in 1547 had passed by unconsolidated. The Protestant cause revived with sufficient energy to force Charles to commit the settlement of religious matters into the hands of an Imperial Diet. Predictably, the Diet's solution, called the Peace of Augsburg, was an anti-Imperial peace which gave each territorial prince the absolute right to decree the religion of his own state. So the Reformation survived with an enormous strengthening of the power of the princes, and Emperor Charles, who wanted for nothing but Imperial and religious unity, was forced to play midwife to intensified German particularism and religious disunity.

# 6

# The Reformation

The Reformation, like the Renaissance, was born in the fold of little states. Indeed, without them, it could not have survived, nor could it have survived without the rivalry of Spain and France. Like the humanists, the Reformers were opposed to the cloister and were thoroughly committed to life in the world. The culture roughly described as humanist, and the Reformation, arose as papal vitality ebbed. Both movements were movements of emancipation, drawing their inspiration and their legitimacy from an earlier period. In their recasting of values, and their attempt to shape new views of man, the humanists and Reformers were akin, but their visions of life and of human capacity and their sources of authority were quite different.

The Reformers were guided by early Christian authority rather than pagan classics. They were less Greek and Roman than Hebrew. While the humanists satirized the abuses of the Church, the Reformers denounced them; the one group tolerated the papacy and concentrated its scorn on superstitions and on the medieval religious orders; the other was alienated by the practice and pretension of the Renaissance papacy. It was not simply that Renaissance popes had been derelict in their duty to cure souls, or that they were politically minded and materialistic, and often guilty of gross nepotism and flagrant immorality. What mattered was the abuse of the spiritual office of the Pope. And the abuse rested on claims that became the focus of the intellectual and theological grievances of the Reformers. By and large

116

the humanists had assumed that they knew the way to salvation and devoted themselves to enriching the possibilities of life, while the Reformers were seeking new avenues to assurance.

### SOCIAL ORIGINS

Behind this quest lay a deep soul-sickness or, perhaps, sensitivity that had continued in Northern Europe alongside the Renaissance. It existed in the country rather than in the gay and elegant court and it shook the middle and lower orders more than the aristocracy.

A sense of doom had lingered long after the Plague. Even during the Plague the reaction in the North had been more hysterical and ghoulish than in the South. Dancing frenzies and flagellations were less frequent in Italy. And one is tempted to attribute this to climate. Throughout the 15th century the North was preoccupied with death, judgment, and hell fire, and an abiding pessimism about man's fate runs through its prose and

Michael Wolgemut, *Death Dance* (Germanisches Nationalmuseum, Nurnberg).

Jan and/or Hubert van Eyck, *The Last Judgment* (The Metropolitan Museum of Art, Fletcher Fund, 1933).

Hieronymus Bosch, detail from *The Garden of Delights* (Museo del Prado).

poetry. A peculiarly macabre dance fashion cropped up, performed by men with skeletons. The dance was intended to remind watchers of their mortality and their equality before the relentless swathe of time. Woodcuts popularized the steps and stages of it. Also, a spate of the early printed pamphlets dealt with the art of dying. In art, morbid undertones took on a bizarre realism. Van Eyck's *The Last Judgment* portrayed the subterranean horror to which the evil were to be committed. Bosch's strange sermons in paint are inhabited by wild, nightmarish creatures. Even Dürer, the realist, flanks his righteous Christian knight on his way to a "city on a hill" with a figure of death holding an hourglass, and a monstrous devil—half wolf, half pig. Similarly, Schongauer's *St. Anthony Tormented by Demons* crawls with hobgoblins and foul friends. Luther believed deeply in the reality and power of Satan and his demons.

As somber as the Northern climate may be, it was also the proximity to death and the frequency of it that kept morbid pessimism alive. In France and Burgundy, for instance, the deso-

Albrecht Dürer, *The Knight, Death and the Devil* (The Metropolitan Museum of Art, Harris Brisbane Dick Fund, 1943).

Martin Schongauer, *Saint Anthony Tormented by Demons* (The Metropolitan Museum of Art, Rogers Fund, 1920).

lation of the Hundred Years War was followed by decimations between rival factions, not to mention recurrences of the Plague. So, from the time of the Plague, through wars, famines, and civil wars, there had been no respite from the threat of death and no guarantee against the onset of disaster.

## MARTIN LUTHER'S PROGRESS TO THE REFORMATION

A high level of death-consciousness was fertile soil for the Reformation, and offers insight into Luther's unusually persistent concern about salvation. For it was the terror of death that sent him into an Augustinian monastery. Born the son of a miner and foundry owner, at Eisleben in Saxony (1483), he did so well in school that his father urged him to become a jurist. He studied arts at the University of Erfurt for four years until, in 1505, a flash of lightning struck him to the ground in a thunderstorm. Without consulting his father he abandoned his intention to go on to law for the robe and cowl. A psychologist, interested in history, has called this Luther's "identity crisis." Then he began to seek a new "life style." These phrases are ways of describing the mystery of conversion.

In the monastery the earlier terror of death became a fearfulness and trembling before God. And his inner torment was not eased by the fact that his father disapproved of his course. Had he done wrong? He felt inadequate to meet the demands of the Mosaic code, let alone Christ's new commandment. The law condemned him. He was a worm in the dust; how could he stand before the Omnipotent Judge? He underwent vigorous austerities to make himself holier, and could not find assurance. An errand to Rome shook him further. He did not notice the glories of the Renaissance or the reminders of antiquity; instead, he saw the worldliness and levity of the clergy, both high and low. He climbed the *Scala Sancta,* 28 stairs, with a Pater Noster and a kiss on each in order to release a soul from purgatory, and at the top he found his faith in the indulgence clouded by doubt. His doubt redoubled on his return. Confession of particular sins seemed inadequate for man's plight. The whole man needed release from total inner corruption. Piece by piece and doubt by doubt, Luther came to view the all-pervasiveness of sin and the only solution that could satisfy his wounded conscience. Since man was too deeply sunk in sin to do anything for his own salvation, he had to be saved, or justified, by faith alone.

Meanwhile he was lecturing on Scriptures and was feeling his way toward a new principle of hermeneutics, a new method of expounding the Word. Like the medieval friars, he abandoned the allegorical and typological approaches to the texts. But unlike the friars, who developed a homilitic style of preaching, Luther concentrated on the inner meaning and underlying unity of Scripture. His attention was fixed on the agony of Christ, forsaken because of the sins of man that He had taken upon Himself. Man could accept his utter worthlessness and yet take joy in the faith that was made possible through Christ's sacrifice. God was a merciful and righteous father, and not a fierce, irrascible judge. The Reformation, one could say, occurred because a brilliant professor was doing his job—preparing thoughtful, original lectures.

### THE REFORMATION

Luther's thoughts tumbled out of the classroom into the marketplace in 1517 when plenary indulgences were being hawked by a Dominican, Tetzel, near Wittenburg. For one-fourth of a florin, buyers were assured that

> As soon as the coin the coffer rings
> The soul from purgatory springs.

Faithful to academic custom, Luther nailed 95 propositions (or theses) in Latin on the door of the castle church as an open invitation to a debate on their merits. They began with a popular attack on the venality of Rome, passed through the doubts as to the Pope's right to remit punishment inflicted by God, and finished by asserting that nothing but contrition could remit spiritual guilt and nothing else was necessary.

Luther's doubts about the extent of the Pope's power to indulge were, indeed, legitimate, for the question had never been definitively settled. Beyond that, however, he had implied an unorthodox way to salvation, and had begun the Reformation.

The press quickly turned his traditional appeal for a debate into an appeal to the people. And, as the debate over indulgences waxed, Luther grew progressively bolder and his criticisms of the Church became more and more fundamental. Finally—after he had been excommunicated—Luther declared that he could not recognize the authority of popes and councils because they had often contradicted each other. He staked his faith and, indeed, his life on Scripture and reason. "Here I stand," he is said to have said at the Diet of Worms (1521), "I cannot do otherwise." His Latin works, published at this time, sold out rapidly.

For a year, Frederick the Wise of Saxony hid Luther in his strongest castle, but meanwhile under the direction of Luther's close friend, Melanchthon, the Reformation in Wittenberg was proceeding. Luther directed it with letters while he translated the New Testament into rich German. Revisions of it and the German Old Testament followed later.

In 1520 he had published three treatises defining his position and calling for action. In the *Address to the Christian Nobility of the German Nation* he appealed to the German ruling classes to throw off the yoke of Rome. He maintained that each believer is his own priest—a doctrine that could yield embarrassing results. Luther meant that any layman could attain forgiveness independent of a priest. The priesthood was only a special vocation. With this stroke, he broke the power of the Church over secular authorities—the power to give or withhold the means of salvation—and encouraged civil authorities to reform an erring church. In *On the Babylonian Captivity of the Church* he attacked the sacramental system, denied four of the traditional sacraments, and kept only Baptism, the Eucharist and, in a revised sense, Penance. Confession was possible between laymen. Marriage was a civil affair to which the Church could give its blessing. Ordination and confirmation were rites of the Church but were not sacraments. Extreme unction was unscriptural and, therefore, was wholly renounced. As for the Eucharist, he wanted both the elements distributed to the laity, denied that it was a reenactment of the sacrifice of the Cross, and deviated from the doctrine of transubstantiation, abandoning the traditional distinction between essence and accident. Christ was in, with and under the elements. Finally, the *Liberty of A Christian Man* set out the doctrine of justification by faith, making faith primary, and a free gift of God, and good works of no heavenly merit but simply the fruit of faith. God, in His mercy, gratuitously declared men just and sinless, men who were, in fact, riven with sin. He would, like a merciful judge, declare the guilty criminal to be not guilty because someone else had made reparation for him. Then the unworthy man could feel free from the terror of God's justice, free from the duress of judgment and death, and live in the joy of an eternal salvation given for no reason of his doing but because Christ's righteousness had been imputed to his credit. Liberty was conceived as a spiritual rather than a political attribute—a liberty, or power, to act righteously—yet, here again, Luther's words were extended to ends that he did not intend. These early writings laid the groundwork for the later additions and subtractions of Reformed theology.

### ANABAPTISM AND THE PEASANTS' REVOLT

The priesthood of all believers was never meant to make every man his own prophet. In several areas (Strassburg, Augsburg, Zurich, and Moravia), separate movements of Christian radicalism developed, some passive, some active. Under the inspiration of radical Lutherans who had turned apocalyptic, the latter sort spread their mystic millenarianism through Germany and the Low Countries, and quoted Luther for support. Unlike Luther, these wanted to bring society, not just faith, under the law of the gospel. Some were even prepared to use force to bring the whole society to purity. Naturally, they attracted the lower classes in town and country. Theirs was a Utopian movement and also a vent for class bitterness. Others were less millenarian, stressing the need to separate the church from worldly society, and emphasizing pacifism and the love-ethic. Luther fulminated against both branches as fiercely as the Catholics, but neither burnings, drownings, nor massacres seemed to halt their spread. Amsterdam caught the enthusiasm around 1530; and in 1534 prophets of the revolutionary wing penetrated the city of Munster to establish the Kingdom of God on earth. The city had just rebelled against its prince-bishop and was in terror of subjection. During a twelve-month siege the Anabaptists instituted a communistic state. Since supplies were running low, this was practical as well as Utopian. Similarly, as the supply of men was depleted by skirmishes, polygamy was instituted for the protection of the womenfolk as well as for personal and unorthodox ethical reasons. To the respectable, this New Jerusalem was an enormity to be crushed and scattered without hint of mercy. Only in this century were the cages containing the bones of the leaders—John of Leyden and Burgomaster Knipperdalling—removed from a steeple where they had swung in derisive display for centuries.

Munster's inglorious defeat cut the heart out of the aggressive branch of Anabaptism, but its pacifist, pietistic aspect continued to conquer the hearts of the downtrodden and dispossessed.

Luther was even more violent in his denunciation of the peasants who demanded "liberty" in social terms on the basis of scriptural authority. The German peasantry were in an ambivalent position in the 16th century. Rising prices were in their favor, but the gap between prices for agricultural produce and industrial equipment was growing instead of decreasing. Not that peasants needed many tools. But their returns were not as large or fast as the city merchant's returns, and the growing disparity was irksome. More trying than this, though, were the downward pressures foisted on them by the Knights and magnates. The Knights as a class were threatened with decline because their rents and services, being relatively fixed, fell behind climbing prices. They were eager to reimpose maximum obligations on a peasantry that was eager to escape them. The Peasants War (1525) was one of a series of agrarian disturbances protesting the injustice and oppression of these landlords. Coming as it did in the early stages of the Reformation, and encouraged as it was in some areas by convinced Anabaptists, it threatened to drown Luther's work in a torrent of civil strife. At first Luther was noncommittal; he recognized that many of the peasants' grievances were genuine, but as the peasants indulged in indiscriminate pillaging he realized the danger to his own cause and turned against them with extraordinary venom. Princes, he urged, could better merit heaven by smiting, slaying and stabbing rebellious subjects than by prayer.

It was said that over 100,000 peasants were killed in battle or executed afterward, and crippling fines were laid upon those who escaped with their lives. From this time the peasantry ceased to count in German politics; princes and magnates had vindicated their power once and for all. Where the revolt had been most vigorous, in Bavaria and Austria, the savage reprisals alienated the peasantry from Luther and the decline of Lutheranism in southern Germany dates from the crushing defeat of the Revolt rather than from the Counter-Reformation.

## LUTHER'S ETHICS

Luther must be considered as a consummate theological politician. His ultimate concerns were inner, yet he had to take political stands to protect the Reformation he desired. Although not excusing them, political needs go far to explain his dubious moral stands on this and other issues. Above all he was fearful for the future, and his siding with the princes was a frank recognition that it was only in their support that the Reformation had any chance of success. Social revolution, chaos, Anabaptism, and even Judaism were threats to the cause that he was swift to denounce. His anti-Semitism was religiously rather than racially determined, but here, as in other matters, he failed to rid himself of the current prejudices of his place and time.

Happily, the dictates of political realism coincided with the ethical consequences of his doctrines. Man was such that he needed the civil sword to contain him in order and tranquility and to bind him in a tolerable state of social cohesion. His liberty was a purely spiritual freedom from the duress of death. It was an inner grace that enabled man to fulfill the law because he had been made righteous by the free gift of God. So Luther preached absolute and unconditional obedience. He refused to condone even passive resistance to the secular arm except by princes. He did nothing to alter the habit of the authoritarian conscience. Indeed, he regarded wicked rulers as God-sent scourges. Lutheranism exchanged obedience to the Pope for abject obedience to the State.

Luther's economic ethics were equally conservative, and in this shared the resentments of his petty bourgeois background. He did not visualize money as a productive thing in itself and therefore forbade all usury. This was to be more medieval than the schoolmen. Like St. Thomas, he believed that each person had his proper place in society and should keep it, and he used the word "calling" to suggest that God wants a Christian to be dedicated to his vocation.

If this was old-fashioned, his appeal to German nationalism was radical and modern, foreshadowing the virulent German-consciousness of the 19th and 20th centuries. The Imperial Knights had early rallied to his standard, prepared to do battle for the emancipation of Germany from the Roman yoke. Although this was one of Luther's themes, his hopes were for peaceful reformation. But his vigorous German style and his outcries against the exploitation of Germany by foreigners were calculated to raise feelings of outraged patriotism.

### LUTHER AND HUMANISM

It was Luther's periodic fury and what seemed to be his reckless rending of the unity of Christendom that alienated the majority of humanists from him. Some, like Melanchthon, were convinced, but most found his convictions hard to stomach because they were held so passionately. The humanists' temper was more urbane. A vast temperamental gulf separated them from the "true believer."

Yet the root of the differences lay in their views of the nature of man and of human destiny. It was no less than the difference between the Renaissance and the Reformation. Erasmus went to the heart of the problem in a tract *On the Freedom of the Will* (1524). Initially he had sympathized with Luther. Had he not also attacked the barren formalism and legalism of the Church, its manifest corruptions, its archaic superstitions, like the veneration of relics? He had also disapproved of the abuse of indulgences, and may be regarded as a forerunner of the Reformation. Nevertheless Erasmus accepted the authority of the Church. He wanted to reform it morally from within, and to trim off its impurities. He was not pressed by desparate doubts to reach out for a new way to salvation. Morals were his concern as salvation was Luther's. Their debate over free will must be taken in a spiritual sense: the free will was not the mundane choosing of this or that during the day. The issue was whether a man could help himself toward salvation by his own voluntary acts. Erasmus thought so, without denying the cooperation of grace in bringing about good works. Luther thought not. Granted that a heathen could be upright and decent, but no man, no matter how pure, was worthy of justification because every human deed was tainted by selfishness and pride. God alone had the freedom to justify whom He chose. One believed that man could, to some extent, make his own destiny, and the other believed that all man could do was throw himself on the love and mercy of God. The difference was insoluble.

## PROTESTANTISM IN GERMANY AND SCANDINAVIA

In an age when such differences mattered more than life, it was inevitable that the Church should encourage the Emperor to root out the Reformation with fire and the sword. Many were burned and executed and, to his dying day, Luther expected to be arrested at any time for trial as a heretic. When he died (1546) he was full of forebodings about the future.

He need not have worried. Although there was precious little idealism in the princes, they had much to gain from the Reformation. They could secularize church property, and they could add the domination of the church to their power over the state, and more than double their influence. These advantages caused several electors and princes to declare for Luther and to impose a local Reformation settlement from above. Territorial churches, subject to the prince, replaced the universal church. When Charles V attempted to force the princes to abandon their caesaro-papistic claims in 1529 they protested, and *Protestant* became the name of all Luther's partisans. In 1531 the dissident princes formed a League of Schmalkald for their mutual defense and, so long as Charles was occupied with Francis and his brother Ferdinand with the Turks, the League held the field. In 1547, during a peace with Francis, Charles defeated the Protestant forces. Yet he could not prevent them from recovering their strength again because of the obstreporous Valois. France and the Turks saved the Reformation in Germany. Finally the Peace of Augsburg (1555) established the principle of princes' choice, and secured Protestantism its future.

By this time, Lutheranism had spread far beyond the German states. Nowhere was the Lutheran Church more of a political creation than in Sweden. Without declaring himself, Gustavus Vasa (1496-1560) found Lutheranism a useful ally in his leadership of the struggle for Swedish independence against Denmark. After his victory and election to the Crown in 1523, Gustavus filled both church and state offices with staunch Lutherans who dutifully preached obedience. He brought church lands under his control in 1527, and then declared himself a Lutheran (1530). From this time his domination of the Church was absolute. Henry VIII of England was to take a page from his book.

In Denmark and Norway Lutheranism flourished with the tacit consent of the King. It spread more from below than above, and by 1536—with the establishment of King Christian on the throne after a civil war with the Catholics—the Lutheran victory was complete. Church ordinances drawn up in the following year have governed the Danish church to the present day. While the Danes did not take Lutheranism undiluted, it was inevitable that their reform movement should assume a Lutheran form in preference to any other. Denmark's lines of communication were direct with Germany and circuitous to the other reform centers. The distance from Rome, as much as the mutual interests of crowns and peoples, accounts for the stability of the Lutheran settlement in Scandinavia.

### THE ENGLISH REFORMATION

English divines hailed Luther as the Father of the Reformation, and so he was, but it is possible to exaggerate his achievement. At the time of his desparate bouts with doubt and despair and his resuscitation in the Christ of the Gospel, there were many who were seeking fresh faith in the scriptures. The Swiss reformer, Zwingli, claimed to have announced the principles of "Scriptures only" and "Justification" before Luther in 1517. The work of the humanist biblical scholars, Erasmus, Reuchlin, and Lefèvre d'Etaples, was pointing in the same direction.

The Reformation was more than one man's conviction; it was a ground swell of religious disaffection. When parishioners were not being offered satisfying spiritual nourishment, the Bible provided it. And this is why the town of Wittenburg did not become the only (or even the leading) center of the Reformation.

Still, Luther had considerable effect on the English Reformation. The first English translation of the New Testament (1526) was done by William Tyndale, an English Lutheran in exile. It was hawked about England by Lollards who, after Wycliffe, had never been completely stamped out. Later, the King's chief minister of the Reformation, Thomas Cromwell, authorized another and complete English translation of the Bible by another English Lutheran, Miles Coverdale (1535). The Boleyn family, whose pretty daughter caught Henry VIII's eye, represented the Lutheran faction at court, and Anne Boleyn's chaplain, Thomas Cranmer, became the Archbishop of Canterbury who finally pronounced Henry's divorce from his first wife. Cranmer's father-in-law was a leading German reformer. In spite of the language barrier, important connections with Lutheranism had been made long before the Reformation occurred in England. The merchants of the Hanseatic League freely imported Luther's works, and his doctrines were discussed by academics at Cambridge and by laymen in London. But, when all is said and done, the English Reformation was the King's and not Luther's business.

Indeed, the King was opposed to Lutheranism. Pope Leo X granted him and his successors the title "Defender of the Faith" for a sturdy defense of the sacraments that Henry had written against Luther in 1521. Luther's reply, which referred to "Henry, King of England, by the disgrace of God," did nothing to mollify him. One reason for Cromwell's sudden fall (1540) was that he tried to enmesh Henry in a Lutheran alliance. Toward the end of his reign, Henry recognized that doctrine was bound to change but, until then, he kept the Church in England well within the folds of orthodoxy—with the exception that he transferred the sovereignty of the Pope to himself.

### THE DIVORCE

He was, then, unmoved by doctrinal considerations; unmoved, too, by the mounting tide of anticlericalism and complaint against the Church. Yet he played on popular resentment and on patriotic sentiment for his own personal and dynastic ends. It is not entirely fair to view Henry's divorce from Catherine of Aragon as a cold and heartless act, since the welfare of his kingdom was involved. His wife had had nothing but a procession of miscarriages and stillbirths after the birth of Princess Mary and the consequences of a female succession could prove disastrous, for treason was never far below the surface. The Wars of the Roses were a living memory, and treason had twice inflamed rebellion in Henry VII's time. By 1525 Henry despaired of a boy from Catherine and began to scour the canon law, the Fathers, and papal decrees for grounds for a divorce. He did have some grounds in law and scripture, because his wife had first been his brother's wife, though that marriage had not been consummated. Moreover, there was hope in that the Pope had granted a divorce to his sister and his brother-in-law for less grounds than he could show.

At this time, or soon after, Henry became infatuated with coquettish Anne Boleyn who had recently returned from the French court. She inflamed his passion by refusing to submit to him. Unsympathetic historians do have some reason for portraying the English Reformation as the illegitimate offspring of a monumental lust. We may wonder why Henry could not have slaked his desire without divorce and remarriage, like other continental monarchs. Either Anne was made of stern stuff, or if she wasn't, the dynastic considerations were preeminent. Through his thoughts and studies Henry had also convinced himself that he was living in sin with Catherine, and all three factors combined to make the divorce the overwhelming single object of his policy.

Regardless of his own judgment of the case, the Pope was in no position to grant a divorce at the time Henry was pressing for it. Catherine was the aunt of Emperor Charles V, and Charles' forces were the masters of Italy. They were then, in fact, occupying Rome itself. How could the defeated Pope shame the family of the victor? By 1529 it was clear in England that the Vatican could never yield to the importunities of the frantic English emissaries. For satisfying one man's familial pride the Pope lost the allegiance of a nation.

### THE SOLUTION

Thomas Cromwell offered Henry the obvious way out of the impasse—the subjection of the Church to the Crown. For eight years (1532-1540) Cromwell was the King's alter ego, his Medieval Justiciar, entrusted with the remaking of the Church in England, and with the remaking of the state accordingly. Cromwell's vision far overreached the King's obsession with divorce and, unlike most politicians. he realized his vision in practice. He established England as a realm with indivisible sovereignty, and the sovereignty he established was not that of the Crown alone, but of the Crown in Parliament. After Cromwell, the Reformation could never be unmade by the King alone, since any change needed the consent of Lords and Commons assembled. Ultimately, the polity, doctrine, and liturgy of the Church fell under the control of Parliament. This solution (neither Lutheran nor Calvinist) has lasted with little interruption ever since.

It was not achieved in a day. First the clergy were intimidated into submission; then the King, with Parliamentary backing, claimed the right to nominate bishops—a right the British Crown still wields—then annates, and above all, appeals to Rome were forbidden. The divorce question could now be "legally" settled in England by the Convocations and pronounced by Archbishop Cranmer (May, 1533). He did so with alacrity because Anne was pregnant and gave birth to Princess Elizabeth four months later.

Having achieved a revolution in church and state, Cromwell guaranteed its permanence by dissolving the monasteries. The profits of their sale went to the Crown, where they were squandered; the land went to the nobility and gentry. In a sense, the dissolutions were a gigantic bribe. And, though doctrine would change and change again, Parliament would never vote to return church land to the church. Thus one permanent effect of the sales was to impoverish the Establishment forever; and indirectly the Crown was impoverished, for instead of conserving its fixed assets, Henry preferred quick sales for immediate gain. Finally the speculative boom in land entwined the interests of landed gentry and urban bourgeois in a peculiarly intimate way to enhance the solidarity of the members of the House of Commons. The future was theirs but, for the moment, the King's power was omnipresent.

As for Anne, she did not live up to her expectations. She could not bear a son and was executed for her failure. Jane Seymour, the next Queen, managed to bring Prince Edward into the world but died immediately afterward. There followed three more marriages whose squalid tales need not be told.

### EDWARDIAN REFORMATION

Just before Henry died, "full of years and sin," he purged his Council of Catholics and left the Duke of Somerset as Protector in charge of the child King Edward VI. Affairs of state became anarchical. Somerset started well-meaning reforms but lacked the acumen to succeed with them, and he alienated the privileged classes by proceeding against enclosers of land and depopulators of villages. The Earl of Warwick overthrew him and, after a time, had him executed for treason. Although Warwick was not a Protestant, he did nothing to halt the forward movement of the Reformation.

Meanwhile, Cranmer had added a doctrinal reformation to the political reformation. He did it in two stages, by measured advance. First, a moderate prayer book (1549) caused some outcry in the West for where Cornishmen spoke neither English nor Latin, Latin was the more familiar tongue. Their rebellion, also economically motivated, was swiftly crushed. A second prayer book of 1552 and 42 Articles of Faith of 1553 were unequivocally Protestant; and these were essentially reinstated in Elizabeth's time. There were slight modifications in the prayer book and the 42 Articles were distilled to 39. In Edward's reign, however, they had little chance for acceptance because the precocious little prince died in 1553.

If England's doctrinal Reformation had occurred alongside its political one, it doubtless would have been less radical than it was. Since Luther's time a host of reformers had arisen, and most of them stood to the left of the originator. Cranmer drew his theology not only from Luther but from what had been before, including Wycliffe, and from Calvin and Bucer and Peter Martyr and Zwingli. An instance of this is the doctrine of the Eucharist. Luther believed he was following the plain words of scripture when he propounded the view that Christ was corporeally present in the bread and wine, yet the bread and wine remained bread and wine still. The divine and the natural coexisted without any transmutation of substance. Cranmer adopted a middle-of-the-road position between Luther and Zwingli, who thought the scriptures plainly showed that bread and wine were mere symbols of Christ's body and blood. Cranmer, like Calvin and Martyr and Bucer, believed that there was a real presence in the elements—a real spiritual presence. Long ago this had been Wycliffe's view, and it can be traced back to the 9th century. Doctrine, then, was thoroughly Protestant, and yet the episcopal structure of the Church remained unchanged. This was the *via media,* or middle way, to which Elizabeth returned in 1558.

### REACTION

Mary overturned it all. She was accepted after Edward's death because she was a Tudor rather than for her Roman Catholicism. Her obsession was to save the state from sin. As long as no attempt was made to restore church lands, Parliament could be rendered pliable. The doctrinal changes were unscrambled, then there began a fierce persecution of Protestants that made Mary abominable to English memory. Not only were hundreds burned in baleful fires at Smithfield near London but Mary prostrated English interests to the interests of her Spanish husband, Phillip II. England was taxed to support the Hapsburg's fight against France—a war in which she had little interest; and England's seamen were forbidden to venture across the Atlantic to disturb the Spanish monopoly in the new world. The affront to national feeling was as harmful to Mary's memory as her intolerance. She died a pathetic woman, loving a husband who did not love her, and hoping to have a child that she could not bear.

During her reign, hundreds of Edwardian Protestants fled abroad. Most of the exiles clung to the second Edwardian prayer book, but those who reached Geneva came away with a sterner theology and a sterner view of church order than they had arrived with.

### ELIZABETHAN SETTLEMENT

Unfortunately for the Genevans, the exiles from Zurich, Frankfurt, and Strassburg reached England before they did. They immediately struck up an alliance with Queen Elizabeth, reinstated the last Edwardian Settlement, and outmaneuvered the Catholics. That staunch alliance between church and state has lasted to this century. The Geneva exiles, not yet called Puritans, were too late to alter the *fait accompli* and spent the next three generations trying to amend it.

One historian called Puritanism the true English Reformation. That is unfair to Anglicanism, but certainly Puritanism brought a new earnestness and energy to the English temper, and its achievements were immense. Puritans led the fight to curb the prerogatives of the Crown and to enlarge the power of the Commons. In the 17th century, Puritans carried liberty and bigotry to New England, and conquered a wilderness. At home they fought their own King and condemned him to a scaffold block. And when their force was spent, and church and crown had been restored, the fame of Puritanism's leaders like Oliver Cromwell lived on, and the works of its poets and preachers, of Milton, Bunyan, and Fox, achieved an earthly immortality that is but a shadow of the unspeakable joy they hoped to have in heaven.

CALVIN AND CALVINISM

Calvin was the source of Puritan vitality, and it is curious that he, the most unbendingly religious of the major reformers, should have had the most secular background. Most leading reformers were priests made over. Calvin was a humanist versed in law. Of course, as a brilliant youngster and son of a Picard lawyer, he had been destined for the Church, but his father later preferred him to take humane and legal studies in Paris, Orleans, and Bourges, which he dutifully did. Everywhere Luther was to be encountered. The head of Calvin's College in Paris was a violent opponent of the new theology, whereas Calvin's Greek teacher at Bourges was a Lutheran proselyte. When Calvin was back in Paris studying Greek and Hebrew, possibly in 1533, he experienced a sudden conversion: the humanist became a reformer.

Late in the year he was driven from Paris and into hiding by the capricious persecutions that were then occurring. He wrote the first and shortest version of his *Institutes of the Christian Religion* while he was at Basle in 1535. When it was published, in 1536, he was taking refuge in Ferrara, but could not stay long. He settled his estate at Noyon and set off for Strassburg via Geneva, where history was lying in wait for him.

Geneva was destined to outshine all other reformed cantons, but at this stage it had just emerged from a nerve-wracking struggle for independence against the Duke of Savoy and its own Bishop. With the help of Protestant Bern, it had secured its independence, and had declared itself in the Protestant camp by suspending the Mass. William Farel had long been trying to induce the city to declare against Catholicism and, sensing his own limitations and Calvin's inner strength, he begged him to stay and help the work. Calvin was reluctant, so Farel predicted that the wrath of God would fall upon him, whereupon Calvin trembled and accepted.

Geneva's precarious independence and the fact that the Reformation had already succeeded in other parts of Switzerland made his task easier. And even before Calvin had arrived, a strict moral regimen had been instituted by the executive or Little Council and approved by the Common Council, made up of all heads of families in the city. This was early in 1536.

Zurich, like the free Imperial City of Strassburg, had embraced reform as early as 1523. Bern followed in 1528 and Basle in 1529. The more populous Swiss cantons soon declared for reform while the larger number remained Catholic. By 1531 the equilibrium was fairly stable.

That year, by the death of Zwingli in an affray against a Catholic force, the Swiss cantons lost their spiritual leader and Zurich lost its preeminent influence. Calvin in Geneva presently wrested leadership from Bern by sheer force of personality.

He brought Geneva a mind utterly untroubled by self-doubt, a frightening presence and a genius for discipline and organization. All along, the success of his Reformation depended on the support of the Councils of Geneva—the Common Council of citizens, the Little Council of 25, the Council of 60, and the Council of 200. The austerity of his regime and his refusal to accept the dictates of the Councils as to the manner in which he should administer sacraments led to his expulsion in 1538. For three years he stayed at Strassburg, learning from Bucer, while Geneva fell prey to factions.

Imminent chaos forced the Councils to recall him and the city's weakness put him in a powerful position; even so, he did not win all the independence of action he desired. By watching and waiting, he so molded the executive Councils that they became more Calvinistic than he. Then Geneva became something like the theocracy he wanted. It was an impressive political achievement, since Calvin never held a civil office.

### CHURCH ORGANIZATION

Discipline was thorough-going and his organization complete. Each city ward had an upright man to oversee its morals and report faults to the clergy. Pastors, teachers, elders, and deacons shared overlapping functions in the church; the pastor was to administer sacraments and preach; the teachers were to instruct the young in true doctrine; elders (nominated by the Little Council) were to have a coeval power with pastors in the running and discipline of the church. Finally, deacons dispensed charitable funds to the sick and needy. Elders and pastors together made up the highest court and policy-making body called the Consistory. Since Calvin's day, this system has been modified. In Scotland, the local church known as the Kirk elected its own elders—the meeting of elders and clergy in a small area was called a Presbytery, for the province it was a Synod, and the supreme gathering was a General Assembly. What distinguished this system from a hierarchy of bishops and priests, or superintendents and pastors, was that the laity, through representatives, participated fully in the administration and policy making of the Church. This was the peculiar genius of Calvin's system. The opportunity for laity to participate made the Calvinist church form (now not limited to Presbyterians) attractive to the respectable and religiously earnest in the Low Countries, Britain, and the New World.

In Geneva this type of organization guaranteed the Church a fair measure of integrity, because it was the substantial citizens who were chosen for elderships, and also it gave the Church direct representation (through these same elders) on the executive councils of the city.

If this interlocking system had not been in force, Calvin may well have been expelled again, for he faced continual opposition from those who ruffled at the over-severe moral discipline of the Consistory—Calvin called these opponents Libertines—and from visiting or resident heretics who were as frequently executed as banished. The Consistory declared them heretics, and the Council decided the punishments.

By 1555 Geneva was in practice, though not in theory, a theocracy. And some liked it that way. John Knox, who reformed Scotland after imbibing Geneva's bracing spirit, found the city "the most perfect school of Christ that ever was since the days of the apostles." Yet after Calvin's death, in 1566, and after Theodore Beza stepped into his shoes, it was said that Genevans did for him for love what they had done for Calvin out of fear and respect.

### THEOLOGY AND ETHICS

Appropriately so, for Calvin's theology was one of fear and respect, rather than love. He followed Luther in his view of man, and even exaggerated the totality of man's perversion after the Fall. Whereas Luther had resolved man's hopeless predicament by faith in the love and mercy of God displayed in Christ, Calvin concentrated his attention on the glory and justice of God. Whether man belonged to the saved or not, his purpose was to worship God and glorify Him forever. Most theologians who believed that God foreknew and forechose those whom he wanted to elect did not like to specify precisely what would happen to the non-elect. Calvin, however, displaying the lawyer's tendency to announce clear and unambiguous categories, propounded a doctrine known as double predestination: a few were chosen for heaven, the rest must surely be damned. And, Calvin thought, it vindicated God's justice that this should be so. His arbitrariness —or rather the arbitrariness he attributed to God—seemed abhorrent to some, and when he was baited on this point he was led into emphasizing the doctrine rather more than he intended. In fact, it was not one of his major doctrines at all and simply an inference from them. Like Luther, he upheld justification by faith, though he could not accept Luther's somewhat mystical view of the Eucharist. Like Luther, and like Zwingli, or Wycliffe or Hus, he was a thoroughgoing scripturalist. He brought the current emphasis on scriptures to a terminal point, short of fundamentalism.

An intense scripturalism and a moral rigorousness marked the Calvinist off from others. Life was a sermon, to be lived for the edification of society, and every precept for living was assumed to be available in scripture. This was a life that could never relax, that was acutely duty conscious, with no heart, little emotion, and no eye for beauty except in the stark. The fellowship of the Church, in communion with living saints, was the only compensation for the loss of soft or romantic longings.

Discipline equipped Calvinism to be the fighting arm of the Reformation. Its belief in the Word (interpreted by Calvin) was as absolute as the Catholic's belief in Church authority. The distinctive organization of Calvinism, partly oligarchic and partly representative, part clerical, part lay, made it proof against the rational unity of a monarchical Church. Bible study was as absorbing as rosary saying, and congregational communion and free prayer were the Calvinists' catharsis for the feeling of sin; as satisfying, apparently, as Penance and Mass were for the Catholic. Calvinism made fewer conversions to Catholicism than any other reform movement.

To describe it as "worldly asceticism" is to forget that the Jesuits were equally, if not more, ascetic and equally committed to the world. Other worldliness was, now, hardly possible. The faith had to be fought for, and monasticism had long since broken down as an ideal under the charges of the humanists before the Reformers attacked it. Calvinists, though strict, enjoyed some pleasures in moderation. They drank wine and cultivated music. Calvinism was neither a new form of monasticism nor a sanctimonious form of worldliness; it was the single-minded pursuit of moral integrity for the greater glory of God.

But God's glory was shown in politics and economics as well as in the Church. Church experience conditioned the Calvinist to participate—or to want to participate—in affairs of state and commerce or in the education of young in right religion. More often than not the Calvinist's business enterprises (following the Church pattern) were communal, joint-stock ventures. And Calvin's attitude toward business was ambivalent: what benefited the community was encouraged; what did not was curbed. Calvin's ethics in every sphere were demanding but were practical and flexible enough to meet every challenge and contingency of life.

## SCOTLAND

Calvinism seeped into France and into Hungary; it conquered Scotland through the fiery ministrations of John Knox. After an adventurous career, Knox became a disciple of Calvin, and returned to Scotland after a stay in Geneva to build an alliance with the nobility against Mary, Queen of Scots. As it happened, Mary, after 1559, became Queen of France when her husband became Francis II. She was an absentee queen, and a French one. Knox played upon Scottish nationalism, on anti-French sentiment, and most effectively on Mary's frivolity. He called her "Jezebel."

Even so, without England's aid the outcome would have been dubious. Elizabeth's intervention in Scotland was a decisive stroke of foreign policy. Having settled her realm into comfortable Protestantism, she realized that a Protestant neighbor would be less troublesome than a Catholic. So English troops and an English fleet were sent north for no other purpose than to help the Scots drive the French out. The English were withdrawn immediately, and within the year (1560) the Reformation was hastily accomplished.

The Scots Confession of Faith was close to the Anglican articles of faith, and their first Book of Discipline allowed for superintendents (bishops or superior clergy) along with a Presbyterian system. At the initial stage the Scots and Anglican churches were not so far apart, though the provision for superintendents was shortly expunged.

Mary returned to Scotland after her husband's death and found that there was nothing she could do. So she devoted her life to torrid love affairs and to a vain pursuit of the English succession. The Scots deposed her in 1567 because she was scandalous and a Catholic, and they crowned James, who was her abandoned child and a Protestant. She took refuge in England where, in spite of herself, she became the focus of plots against Elizabeth that cost her her life.

Pockets of Catholics remained in Scotland's Highlands which is not surprising—and pockets remain there, even now, of Presbyterians who live as strictly as Genevans must have done under Calvin.

### CALVINISM AND CAPITALISM

There is a theory that Protestantism, and especially Calvinism, was a great fillip to the rise of capitalism. To a large extent the argument hinges on what, precisely, is meant by capitalism. If it is individualism that is considered, then Calvinism was less individualistic than congregational and regimented. If it is the rationalizing of business organizations, then Calvinism is not especially rational, and perhaps less so than a hierarchical system. Its ethics are considered to be conducive to money making, but without other qualities, thrift, sobriety, and industry seldom make large fortunes. Scotland is the glaring example. Capitalism relies on a variety of ingredients in a variety of combinations for a variety of enterprises. Prodigality is often as rewarding as miserliness; adventurousness is as rewarding as care; and a lax morality is no less appropriate than moral restraint. A capacity for hard work and a devotion to the pursuit of wealth can flourish in any confession. Far more important for success than religion is accessibility to rich resources and the wealthy markets. While connections can fruitfully be drawn between religion and the social context, the Reformation was not the simple reflex of an economic movement, nor was capitalism its illegitimate child. The Reformation was a spiritual chapter in man's endless theodicy; a new stage in his search for self-illumination.

# 7

# The Catholic Reformation and the Counter-Reformation

Times occur in history when mortal dangers are clearly perceived but nothing is done to avoid or minimize them. The Reformation was such a time for the Roman Catholic Church and one cannot but wonder why no shift was made to meet the heresy spreading like wildfire across the North. Past experience had not fitted the Renaissance Papacy to meet the challenge. Its concerns were local. Rome badly needed beautification and Italian politics were all-absorbing; the civil arm could extirpate the heretics.

Such confidence was misplaced, for while the Emperor was a devoted Catholic, in the last resort he would rather close and bar the doors of Milan to the French than disperse the Lutherans. Politics, to the politician, came first; the semblance of power was holier than holy faith.

Confidence in the powers that be was also misplaced because any political counterthrust to the Reformation needed to be girded with righteousness. Troops alone could never conquer; they needed the reinforcement of a thorough reexamination of doctrine and church administration. This need was deeply felt by some pious souls, if not by the popes.

143

## CATHOLIC REFORM

Even before Luther had attacked the sale of indulgences, a mystical and moral revival was beginning to develop in the South. Savonarola of Florence is a striking example. He came as a notable Dominican preacher to St. Mark's cathedral in 1491 and quickly established himself as a visionary, a prophet of deaths and destructions, and also as a dedicated defender of the liberties of the citizens against the Medici. After the defeat of Pietro de Medici by Charles VIII and that French king's withdrawal from the city, in 1494, Savonarola became the lawgiver and virtual dictator of Florence. His doctrines, his unbending rigidity and strictness, and his bold denunciations of Rome's and the Pope's corruptions brought down a bull of excommunication upon his head. Yet he continued to organize the youth and to encourage the citizenry in various religious austerities and celebrations. On one occasion, in 1497, under the influence of his intense charisma, the townspeople disgorged their "vanities"—dice, trinkets, ornaments, cosmetics, false hair, and lewd literature—for public burning. This carnival was repeated just before his fall in 1498. Although the Medici faction desired and the Pope contrived his destruction, it was the fickle mob who stormed his convent and carried him off from the church to an intimidated and hostile signory. Fearfully tortured, subjected to a mockery of a trial by commissioners who had been ordered by the Pope to sentence him to death, "even were he a second John the Baptist," he was ceremonially degraded then hung on a cross between two disciples. Crosses and bodies were then burned to the delight of the crowd. Tired of purity and moral earnestness the populace had found that Savonarola too, like a vanity, was expendable. Meanwhile, in a Parthian shot just before his death, the monk prophesied the calamities that would befall the city under Pope Clement. To this day, flowers are strewn on the day and on the spot that he died.

However, Florence had had but a brief flurry of piety under Savonarola. His movement did not rekindle the zeal of the Dominican order, nor, indeed, make any lasting impact outside the city. More lasting and more effective was the forming of a nonmonastic devotional group called the Oratory of Divine Love (founded 1497). It included laymen as well as priests, and from its numbers in Rome came a clutch of outstanding cardinals. The Oratory spread spontaneously throughout the length and breadth of Italy, taking hold amongst the cultured, and weaning them away from cynicism. Paul III, himself a nepotist, had the vision to ask members of this group to prepare for him a report of the state of the Church in 1538. The report did not mince words; it lashed the papacy by naming every vice and scandal, even to the prostitutes who milled about St. Peter's attended by clerics—presumably not for the care of their souls. Protestants made great sport of it.

One outgrowth of the Oratory was a new order that lived under a rule though not in a monastery. In 1524 the Pope sanctioned the Order of Theatines who were dedicated to maintaining high standards among ordinary clergy. Another new group—the Capuchins—tried to recapture the pure idealism and evangelistic fervor of St. Francis of Assisi. By 1619 they numbered 1500 houses.

These and lesser orders were responses to the Renaissance and not counters to the Reformation. Similarly, the rise of mysticism in Spain was an indigenous development owing nothing to the growth of Protestantism elsewhere. Many of the more enthusiastic mystics, alight and afire with their dreams, fell under the suspicion of the Inquisition. The most famous of them was St. Theresa of Avila (1515-1582), a shrewd organizer whose deep religious experiences were so affecting that they made her ill. She founded a number of monasteries and nunneries in obedience to her visions, and her young disciple, St. John of the Cross (1542-1591), reformed others. His poetry expressed the quintessence of the mystic spirit in lofty cadence and sublime imagery. These saints belong to the long tradition of those who have heightened the spirituality of the Church, and owe little or nothing of their drive to the pressure of Protestantism.

### COUNTER-REFORM: LOYOLA AND THE JESUITS

The counter-Reformation developed during the mystic revival in Spain and was led by Ignatius Loyola, a soldier before he was a mystic. His chances of a life-long military career were ruined by a bullet wound in the hip, and as he recuperated his enforced idleness and his new-found reading matter—lives of the Saints and of Christ—redirected his mind and talents toward the service of the Church. He spiritualized his earlier experience as a knight; the Virgin became his lady; and he envisioned the Christian progress as a continuing military campaign. His Christianity was medieval and chivalric.

But first he became a hermit (1522) and saw a vision that confirmed his faith. He began to write the *Spiritual Exercises* at this time, though they were not published until 1548. A source of inspiration to which Jesuits return again and again to this day, they begin with a contemplation of man's sinfulness, move to consideration of Christ's struggle against evil, then to the Passion and finally to the joy of the believer joining God. To participate in the *Exercises* is an agonizing, compelling, cleansing, and spiritually renewing experience.

After a pilgrimage to Jerusalem, Ignatius decided that he needed education to increase his influence; first he attended grammar school with young boys, then went on to the University of Toledo. After a time his enthusiasm earned him the suspicion of the Inquisition and he thought it prudent to continue his studies in Paris. By strange coincidence he arrived at the college that Calvin had attended just months after Calvin's departure. Already he had five Spanish disciples and now he attracted four Frenchmen to him. Returning to Spain for theology, the band decided on a pilgrimage to Jerusalem, but war and politics preventing them, they met in Rome to beg for Papal approval for a new order. They won it in 1540.

The Society of Jesus was organized on quasi-military lines. Its ranks, in ascending order, were novices, Scholastics, and the Professed of the Four Vows, who elected the General of the Order for life. To the usual vows of chastity, poverty, and obedience, Loyola added a fourth vow of absolute obedience to the Pope. By the Bull of 1540 Jesuits were charged to hear confession, to teach, and to preach. Thus was formed a clerical body more disciplined than the Calvinists, more flexible, and more highly centralized. Like the Calvinists, the Jesuits did not shun the world, but embraced it in order to lead it to higher truth and sanctity.

What success did they have? At first their education was restricted to their own novices and scholastics, but they soon offered schooling to the laity, and it was so effective that it became their enemy's chief ground against them. Their preaching raised standards in pulpits throughout the Church, and their catechisms instructed millions of youngsters in the doctrines of Trent.

The reclamation of Poland from Protestantism was their signal achievement. They had three advantages over the divided and leaderless Protestants. Their leader, St. Peter Canisius, was in every way remarkable. He had the ear and the heart of the King. And the Jesuits' educational system was better than its rival's. Although Poland's backward social structure may not have been conducive to the growth of Calvinism, Lutheranism might have succeeded with royal support. But it was unthinkable that Ferdinand, Charles V's brother and later Emperor, would turn his back on his family's traditional policies—the twin goals of regaining souls for the Church and land for the Hapsburgs.

Finally Jesuit missions, led by St. Francis Xavier, revitalized the Church's missionary endeavor. Jesuits were not the only missionaries, of course. Carmelites pushed into Persia, and Franciscans into California, but at this early stage the Jesuits stood in the van. Xavier died in Japan. Others penetrated into India, China, and Peru. By the time of Loyola's death in 1556, there were 1500 members of the Society and they had studded the globe with enclaves of missionaries.

COUNCIL OF TRENT

Yet the church's spiritual and evangelical revival would have lacked force without theological and administrative reform. Although the need was obvious enough, the obstacles in the way of calling a reforming Council were immense. Not only were clergy of laxer habits opposed to it, but even purer souls, members of the Oratory of Divine Love, felt that reform should come from below and from the heart, rather than be legislated from above. Political dissension was the prime obstacle: a Council was called in 1536 but the war between France and Spain kept it from meeting until 1545. By then it was too late to nip Protestantism in the bud.

Secular political rivalries were compounded by ecclesiastical politics. Since the attempted Conciliar revolution of the 15th century the popes' dread of Councils had not abated. So the Council was ordered in such a fashion that papal power would not be lessened. The votes in the Councils of the 15th century had been by national delegation; but at Trent the abbotts and theologians were excluded from power. The vote was given to bishops and heads of orders, and their majority was to be binding. Needless to say, there were many more Italian than non-Italian bishops and the Italians could be counted on to maintain papal supremacy.

The choice of Trent, too, was a political compromise between France and the Empire. Also it was sufficiently close to Italy to attract a full turnout of Italian bishops. Even so, the Pope would have liked the Council to deliberate closer to home, and he took advantage of an outbreak of plague in Trent to suggest removing it to Bologna—in papal territory. Charles V, however, ordered his bishops to remain in Trent and the first session of the Council ended in deadlock. A new pope allowed the calling of another session early in 1547, and a third session in 1562 and 1563 was called by a pope wholeheartedly dedicated to reform. Pius IV (1559-1565) had been a member of the Oratory of Divine Love. But he was not above politics. He hated the Spanish in general and Charles V in particular, and was not prepared to concede to the far-reaching reforms advocated by the Spanish bishops. Among other things, they would have liked the authority of Councils declared superior to that of popes.

Bitter controversies and intrigue permeated every session. The political outcome, however, was assured by the predominance of the Italians—of the 255 prelates who signed the official Acts of the Council, 189 were Italians. Thus any revolutionary Conciliar stirrings were beaten before they had begun. The immediate result of the Council was a tremendous boost to papal prestige. Ultimately the outcome of Trent was the dogma of Papal Infallibility, defined in 1870.

Theologically speaking, the Council ended all possibility of union with Protestants and it closed the door to much of the rich theological speculation of centuries past. While it may be true that the Council drew upon the best of its tradition, drawing heavily on St. Thomas Aquinas, it is also true that the breadth and flexibility of medieval Catholicism were summarily abandoned. The Church became more intolerant theologically as it grew more authoritarian politically. This, perhaps, is in the nature of powerful institutions beset by powerful challengers.

### INDEX AND INQUISITION

The *Index* was drafted and the Inquisition came into its own. The *Index* (1558) was a list of books prohibited in whole or in part to the ordinary Roman Catholic. At first, all of Erasmus' works were among those condemned, but later this indiscriminate sentence was modified. It is a tribute to the power of the printed word that books should seem such dangerous emissaries of heresy that they merited repression. Both the *Index* and the office of Inquisitor were abolished by Vatican II in 1966.

Once the instrument of medieval Spanish rulers, the Inquisition was also constituted in Italy as the Roman Inquisition in 1542. That it was pathologically afraid of heresy, that it was sinister and occasionally cruel, that its procedures were unfair, and that it was drastically effective, none deny. It literally burned out the small pockets of Protestantism in Spain and in Italy. No one except the Pope was free from suspicion: the Archbishop of Toledo was swallowed up for a 17-year trial and forced to abjure certain errors. Even St. Ignatius Loyola and St. Theresa of Avila fell under suspicion. The Inquisition proved more powerful in Spain than in Italy because it had firmer support from above, from the king, and perhaps from below as well. In Italy it long continued to function, arresting Galileo in the 17th century and the great lover, Casanova, in the 18th century but, by then, its main work had been accomplished.

Harsh as it may seem, the Inquisition was the Roman Catholic equivalent to the purges of their lands by Lutheran princes, and to the unbending discipline of Geneva's Consistory and Little Council. When heresy was considered damnable, death at the stake, or by drowning or strangling seemed a kindness. Fire, sword, water, rope, torture, and terror were not too drastic to root out the virus of sin. From this point of view the Inquisitors were being cruel to incorrigible sinners, only to be kind to the Catholic majority. In cases of hallucination, witchcraft, and sexual perversion they showed a good deal of restraint and common sense.

## TRENT AND DOCTRINE

If the *Index* and the Inquisition were alien to the spirit of the Renaissance, the theological settlements of the Council of Trent, in part at least, enshrined the Renaissance philosophy of man. On the questions of justification by faith and predestination the Council emphasized the freedom of man and his potential for divine endeavor. He could prepare himself for faith and co-operate with it, while being insufficient without grace for salvation. Man lived neither in absolute freedom nor in total bondage. Thus the Council managed to preserve human integrity and responsibility as well as the might and mystery of grace.

The Council was equally unconciliatory to Protestantism in other matters. Whereas Protestants revered tradition only insofar as it conformed with scriptures, the Council distinguished scripture and tradition and placed both on an equal footing as sources of authority. Transubstantiation was judged to be the only permissible doctrine of the Eucharist: no quarter was given to Protestant views. The seven sacraments were reaffirmed, indulgences were declared effective and a proper adjunct to the Pope's power to redistribute merit. Although Protestants ever so stoutly denied it, Trent threw the weight of its authority in favor of the existence of purgatory, and claimed that intercession and the sacrifice of the Mass helped those souls detained there. Finally, in the Tridentine Profession of Faith of 1546, to this day recited by all bishops and beneficed clergy and imposed on all converts, there was a vow of obedience to the Roman Pontiff.

The dogmas of Trent reflect the wisdom that the 16th century Roman Church found most acceptable in its past—wisdom sharpened by the witness of what seemed to be the errors of the Protestants. Catholics are bound to accept what this Council defined—to reject any Tridentine dogma is heresy. So thorough and exhaustive was its doctrinal analysis that even the recently promulgated dogmas of the Immaculate Conception (1854) and of the bodily Assumption of the Virgin (1954) were foreshadowed in a decree of Trent that exempted Mary from the otherwise universal taint of original sin. Trent, then, was a consolidation and codification of Roman faith, expressing the conscience of the upper hierarchy of that time and remaining a touchstone and repository of Roman Catholic truth down to the present age.

### ADMINISTRATIVE REFORM

For all its troubles and tribulations, Trent's achievements were stupendous. Exhaustive administrative reforms accompanied its doctrinal utterances: assaults were made on nonresidences and the holding of a plurality of benefices and against lax, corrupt, immoral, or unchaste clergy. The Pope was implored to choose cardinals worthy of their dignity, and all religious orders were subjected to a regulatory code. Seminaries were proposed for the education of priests, so that the Renaissance humanists' favorite butt, the unlearned priest, could be pushed into the past. Princes were commanded not to interfere with Church affairs and property, while laymen were ordered to attend Mass regularly. In short, the whole fabric of the Church was refurbished, no corner and no quarter went uncleansed, no level and no rank escaped fervent prescription and exhortation.

Happily for the Church, the duty of implementing the decrees of Trent fell to the austere Pope Pius V (1566-1572), the first pope in half a millenium whom the Church considered worthy of canonization. An uncompromising man, he punished disobedience with severity. He was as strict on himself as with others, visiting barefooted like a pilgrim in his diocese, praying and fasting at length. Also he reformed the curia, had the police rid the streets of prostitutes, and cleared the papal palaces of moveable pagan nudities, to the infinite benefit of the Capitoline Museum. He looked and behaved a little like Calvin.

Under Pius V a new Catechism, Breviary (daily service book), Missal (mass book), and translations of St. Thomas' *Summa* were published. These new works contributed greatly to the unification and clarification of doctrine. The Missal replaced the four permissible modes of celebration and remains virtually unchanged today, though a new mass is now being used in some areas, which is new in form—in vernacular, for instance—and, implicitly, in theology.

Under the divisive stresses of Protestantism and nationalism it is quite possible that Catholicism may have disintegrated without Pius V and the Council of Trent: the Inquisition would have had less clearly defined principles to act upon and the impetus to reform might have been lost in a thousand individual directions. With Trent behind it, Catholicism took heart. Its hopes for re-uniting Christendom began to flow again; a perfervid crusading spirit began to grip Church leaders and Catholic monarchs alike. Yet their hopes and dreams were dreamed too late. One result of the definition of dogma—no matter how valuable it was for the Roman Church—was that Protestantism could never come to terms with it on the basis of the Tridentine Settlement. The gulf had become unbridgeable, yet the Church ardently believed that it could fly the gap, occupy the Protestants' domains, and trans-form their spirits. Both sides, in fact, suffered under the delusion that they could overturn the social, political, and spiritual cir-cumstances that had given rise to the deep division. Rivers of blood would flow before the impossibility of these misappre-hensions would be accepted. Ironically, the Council of Trent completed its monumental labors in 1563, the same year that England issued its Protestant 39 Articles of Faith. The coinci-dence testifies that just as the Roman Church had finally and effectively prepared itself for battle against apostasy the Protes-tant camp was stronger than ever.

## SPAIN AND THE NETHERLANDS

In the East and in the Empire the arrival of heathen Turks and Protestants had been accepted as inevitable. But in the West the hope that Protestantism could be brought to an uncondi-tional surrender continued to bedevil the policies of Spain and France.

For Phillip II, heir to all of Charles V's Spanish dominions, religion and national motives were one. He saw no distinction between the good of the Church and the interest of the state. He was a devoutly religious person whose prayers and fasting were legendary. His palace, unlike that of any other contempo-rary ruler, was partly a monastery so that it might give glory to God as well as grandeur to the Crown.

Yet he would suffer no slur upon his majesty, and his relations with the popes were not always amiable. He disapproved of the Jesuits on his own territory because their loyalty to the Pope seemed to compromise their loyalty to him. Through the Spanish Inquisition and through his ecclesiastical appointments he exerted a control of the Church fully as powerful as that of Henry VIII.

Unlike Henry, Phillip was austere and less effective. He was the arch bureaucrat who pored day and night over his papers. His solemn marginal comments appear beside the significant and trivial alike, and, in truth, he was not able to distinguish the one from the other. His days were burdened with religious exercises and political busywork so that he lost his distance and his perspective on larger affairs.

Bureaucrat that he was, he began a drastic centralization of power in the Netherlands and rode roughshod over the customary privileges of the provincial nobility. Theirs had formerly been the right to advise the Regent, but henceforth only a Council of three was to do so, and both Regent and Council were to be closely supervised from Spain. Although economical and rational in theory, this pruning of power was politically disastrous.

And to compound the offense, Phillip II proposed a thoroughgoing reform of the Church which, by reorganizing dioceses and recalling all ecclesiastical nominations to the Spanish Crown, would rob the nobility of the powers and preferments that they had come to look upon as adjuncts to their rank. In many ways a splendid reform, when coupled with the political centralization it doubled the fears of the Netherlandish nobility for their privileges. Furthermore, the proposal to reform the Church discomforted the laxer clergy and united the Protestants—formerly divided—who feared that reform would cut much of the ground from under their feet.

Protestantism became a rallying point of Netherlandish dissent. It was one source of opposition that touched all classes down to the various Anabaptist and sectarian enthusiasms of the urban proletariat. But it must be said that Protestants were a minority in every province—at least at the outset. What mattered initially was the particularistic claims of the nobility, wanting their privileges guaranteed in full. The story of the revolt is one of the change and broadening of a narrow, selfish, aristocratic protest into a national movement of liberation.

Phillip's inconsistency and his inability to diagnose the cause of the trouble encouraged the opposition. Foremost among them was William the Silent, Prince of Orange, Count of Nassau, who had once been a trusted servant of the Spanish Crown and diligent in its service, but who was now quick to respond when constitutional and ecclesiastical centralization threatened his power. His marriage to a Lutheran in 1561 marks the beginnings of his religious progress away from Spain. Twelve years later he professed a moderate Calvinism. Whatever his motives to begin with, by the time of his death William envisaged a united and independent Netherlands with a representative—though not democratic—form of government. His indomitable resolve and resilience inspired the Netherlanders to defy, and at times even to defeat, the most colossal power of Europe whose armies had not previously been beaten in the century.

At first Phillip made all the concessions that were demanded, but he would never yield the reform of the Church. Those of the nobility who importuned his regent were sneeringly dismissed by a loyalist as "Beggars." Yet it was not the nobility but the middle and lower classes of the cities who began the train of violence by a spree of image smashing and church sacking. This sacrilege ended the policy of royal concessions and temporizing. Phillip sent the Duke of Alva to crush the violators without mercy. Alva's reign of terror might well have succeeded if it had not been accompanied by a new and oppressive system of taxation. Among other taxes, a proposed 10 percent purchase tax provoked a universal reaction. Alva was unable to levy it. Instead of isolating the Protestant rebels, the Duke had identified Protestantism with a national economic apprehension.

Nevertheless, the armed protest, by now quite openly led by William the Silent, fared badly. Alva began a systematic mopping-up of the cities, but the sea, it seemed, was Protestant. A group of ruffians, calling themselves "Sea Beggars" and flying the colors of Orange, captured the port of Brill (1572), and unsettled Phillip's confidence in his governor. So the ruthless but effective Alva was replaced by a more conciliatory and less brutal governor and the offending proposal of a purchase tax was withdrawn.

The success of Spain's campaign on land continued, but the dramatic exploits of the Sea Beggars, strategically less important, were psychologically more damaging to Phillip's cause. They captured Middleburg from the sea. And when the city of Leyden was succumbing under a rigid siege, William managed to induce the land-owners roundabout to agree to a cutting of the dykes twenty miles away. It was done; the salt sea flowed in and the Spanish troops dragged themselves from Leyden through the mud. Barges floated supplies and reinforcements to the city; and as the tide turned, the wind backed up the waters and the dykes were built again. To commemorate the miracle, William founded the University of Leyden (1574).

But one relief was not a victory, and the Spanish continued to gain ground despite the disaster known as the Spanish Fury. Underpaid Spanish troops, quartered in Antwerp, mutinied and ran amok in 1576, sparing neither age nor sex, creed nor nationality. The city was reduced to a shambles. "Within nine days," wrote a contemporary, "Antwerp, which was one of the richest towns in Europe, had now no money nor treasure to be found therein, but only in the hands of murderers and strumpets." Catholics and Protestants were united in horror, but an astute political move effaced the ill effects of the Fury. A *Perpetual Edict* capitulated to the original demands of the opposition: promising a full restoration of ancient constitutional liberties and the withdrawal of Spanish troops. Fifteen of the seventeen provinces, except Zeeland and Holland who viewed it as a trick, accepted the terms of the Edict.

Zeeland and Holland were in dire peril. The governor attacked, thus publishing abroad his own faithlessness in the Edict, and having destroyed mutual good faith, he died. In the lag of time between one death and the arrival of another governor—the Duke of Parma—Zeeland and Holland persuaded other provinces to their view.

In the North, Protestantism had increased in influence and swelled in numbers because it had been so closely identified with the liberation struggle and because thousands of Southerners had

migrated from the Spanish-held territories. Naturally, they stiff-
ened the spirit of resistance wherever they settled.

Despite this crystallizing religious cleavage, William still hoped
to hold all the provinces, united, to the goal of independence.
Events, however, moved beyond him—seven Northern provinces
founded a Union of Utrecht, and the Southern provinces formed
a Union of Arras. The South was prepared to be loyal on the
conditions of the earlier Edict, and Parma, wisely, acceded. These
provinces henceforth remained in Spanish possession. After 1713
they passed to Austria, and after 1830 achieved independence as
the state of Belgium. Politically versatile, and militarily brilliant,
Parma's success drove William, in desperation, to ask for French
aid. It proved a fiasco. He was seeking another source of support
when he was felled by the pistol shot of a devoted supporter of
Spain. His last thoughts were of his people. "My God, have pity
on these poor people," and the inscription on his grave asserts
that he valued the fortunes of the Netherlands above his own. At
the news of his death people wept in the streets.

William's son, Maurice of Nassau, now led the forces of the
Northern provinces. Following William's last inclinations, the
States-General begged Elizabeth of England for aid, and after a
long hesitation she dispatched soldiers under an incompetent
commander. They boosted morale at first, but proved a lingering
failure.

Why could not Parma overrun the North? The English helped
to check his advance. But, more importantly, geography was
against him. Canals, marshes, lakes, and rivers formed a fence
just south of Zeeland. Therefore, his most successful line of
attack was from the East, and here he encountered the stiff
defense of Maurice.

Spain, meanwhile, was syphoning off its resources to mass a
gigantic offensive against England. This conquest was certainly
more ephemeral than that of the Netherlands, and in pursuing it
Spain lost in both theatres.

After the death of Parma (1592), Maurice reconquered the
Northeastern provinces and his power enabled him to establish
Reformed religion once and for all in seven provinces. In a real
sense, the religious cast of the North was both a contributing
cause and a consequence of war.

Finally it was of paramount importance that Zeeland, and Holland—the two central provinces of the coast—had been rid of military campaigning since 1576. Thus, shipbuilding and the fishing industries were allowed to develop without interruptions. Their trade and wealth filled the bellies of the Northern armies. Their ships patrolled the seas, and never lost control of the river Scheldt. So they cut off Antwerp's access to its hinterland and helped to impoverish it. Moreover, their control of the sea bound the Spaniards to a lopsided offensive on land only. The herring trade—one of the staples of European commerce—continued to boom and an international trade radiating from Amsterdam spread prosperity in the wake of Maurice's forces. The United East India Company was founded in 1602. Amsterdam replaced Antwerp as the commercial hub of the Northeast. Hence, though it is only part of the story, there is truth in the quip that the humble kipper brought low the pride of one nation and made another.

A truce was drawn in 1609. Phillip II had died in 1598, leaving Phillip III, with credit impaired, a fast-vanishing supremacy, and nothing to do but make peace. The struggle was not yet done; but the splitting of the Netherlands, which some consider an unnatural division, was to prove lasting.

### SPAIN AND ENGLAND

England's minor and not altogether creditable role in the Revolt of the Netherlands was responsible for bringing the full wrath of Phillip II upon it. He determined (1585) to conquer England, to win her for Spain, and to wean her from apostasy.

That Elizabeth had managed to avoid a war thus far by diplomacy alone was something of a feat; that she interfered in the Netherlands seemed foolhardy. It was an egregious act of war, and England's only defense was the Channel. Her population was even smaller than that of the 18 United Provinces, and the government's annual income was a pittance compared to the revenues that Spain drew, not from taxes, but from imported treasure alone.

The Enterprise of England, as Phillip called it, was something of a crusade. It received the cautious blessing of the Pope—Elizabeth was a heretic and the Bull of Excommunication had been issued against her in 1570—yet the Pope rightly suspected that not only souls for the Church but the Crowns of England and Scotland were the prize.

England's plans were flexible and pragmatic, while Spain's were ponderous. Phillip planned to dispatch a mighty Armada with a huge invading force aboard, and never veered one degree from this strategy. Elizabeth was inclined to wage a Channel battle; her sea dogs, Sir William Hawkins and Sir Francis Drake, who had learned their skills in illicit trading and piracy along the Caribbean, were all for waging a global war, both in the Channel and across the Atlantic, attacking the colonies and cutting off Spain's treasure supply. In fact, English strategy was a hodgepodge of notions tailored none too well to the opportunities. Elizabeth always hoped that English expeditions would return with a profit as well as a victory, and given her straightened circumstances one can hardly blame her.

Phillip began to assemble his fleet in Cadiz, only to be set back a year by a daring raid by Sir Francis Drake (1587), who called it singeing the King of Spain's beard. That daredevil sailed into the harbor, sank 30 ships, destroyed naval supplies, and temporarily dislocated Phillip's prestige and his credit. Temporarily only, for within a year the Armada sailed; 130 ships, bound for the Netherlands for more soldiers and supplies from Parma before delivering its blow to England. Meanwhile, death had carried off Spain's finest Admiral and there was no experienced man to replace him.

In size the fleets were fairly evenly matched, and they were equally ill-provided for. But in sailability and firepower the English were superior. Hawkins had reorganized the English Navy, concentrating his building on fast maneuverable ships with long-range guns so that English fighting ships could sail rings around the stately Spanish galleons. Hawkins hoped to win by seamanship and accurate gunnery, while the Spanish tactics were to come alongside and board with soldiers. Spanish seaman were but seascouts for the troops, and their ships were huge rafts on which what was essentially a hand-to-hand land engagement was to be fought.

The Armada left Corunna to sail northward in a crescent-moon, line-abreast formation that stretched seven miles across the sea. When they were sighted off the southern coast of England, the main English fleet was bottled up in Plymouth harbor by a contrary wind. At this point, if instructions had permitted, the Spanish might have entered and destroyed the English in the confines of the harbor. But inflexible orders prevented such a diversion. Also the Spanish had no idea that the main fleet was in there. So the English rowed and towed their ships to open sea and began a running battle lasting for nine days up the Channel.

Spanish defense was remarkable, for though the fleet sustained damage at no time was its tight formation broken. The disaster came only when the formation was broken open after it had put into port at Calais. For after the Spanish anchored behind the sands, the English sent in fire ships during the night, causing panic and forcing the Spanish to cut their cables and drift out into the sea. In the morning they were seen to be scattered and the English were able to use their advantages to devastating effect. In several hours' bombardment the Armada was crippled. Even so, the Spanish Admiral managed to restore the fleet to order and move northward. His valiant efforts were nullified by the wind, for a storm completed what the English had begun, driving the Spanish up the Channel followed by English ships whose ammunition was long since exhausted. Doubling through the islands north of Scotland, the Armada ran into the Atlantic gales that flung tens of ships and thousands of soldiers upon the rocky isles and inhospitable shores of Scotland and Ireland. Sixty-seven vessels returned. Ten thousand soldiers had drowned or otherwise perished. England struck a medal bearing the motto "Afflavit Deus, et dissipati sunt"—God blew and they were scattered—but, in fact, the defeat had occurred off Calais before the squall had struck. English prowess became the stuff of legend.

Although it was a fearful defeat, the threat from Spain remained ever-present. England's offensive degenerated into a series of publicly supported privateering ventures, while Spain was rebuilding the Armada. England was to enjoy only one other resounding success, when Sir Walter Raleigh led English seamen into Cadiz in 1596—as Drake had done before. In a brilliant engagement they captured and sacked the city. And the loot covered the cost of the venture. In swift retaliation, Phillip loosed a new

Armada from Lisbon, ninety ships strong. No sooner had it reached Cape Finisterre (1598), en route to Ireland (in all probability), than a gale wrecked half the vessels on the shore, and the remainder beat back to Lisbon where the seasick soldiers deserted as fast as they could. England's later ventures were equally fruitless and ill-managed. Although Spain made a last attempt to turn the tables, sending troops to aid an Irish rebellion, in imitation of Elizabeth's support in the Netherlands, the war grew cold. Phillip died dreaming of a third Armada. A desultory truce reigned, the fiery spirits were becalmed, and peace was finally signed in 1604, the year after Elizabeth's death.

Phillip and Elizabeth were striking contrasts, the man a fond father, the woman at times a waspish spinster. The King was imperturbable, phlegmatic, and melancholy; while the Queen was both imperious and petty, pretty and gay. Elizabeth never aimed higher than the possible and worked to her ends with every trick and skill and every charm she could muster. Phillip piled grand design on grand design and squandered his patrimony in the process. While she was often dilatory, he was immovable in his resolves; she left bureaucratic details to her faithful councillors; Phillip carried the whole burden on himself. Like so many Europeans since and before him, he was haunted by the vision of a united Europe, united in faith and obedience, but he could never realize the dream for all his prodigious, if pedestrian, industry.

Both loved their countries dearly, presiding over golden ages of art, literature, music, and adventurous endeavor. One served with charm and regality, the other with prayer and devotion. As it turned out Elizabeth's pragmatism triumphed over Phillip's vision of a world without the Reformation. It was bound to be so because his vision was impossible.

### RELIGIOUS WARS IN FRANCE

Spain, England, and the Netherlands staged epic conflicts for posterity while France, in her religious wars, offered no grandeur of design, little unity of purpose, and few hints of noble action in high places.

Persecution of the French Protestant had been fitful under

Francis I (d. 1547) and Henry II (d. 1559). These two had been more bitterly opposed to the Emperor than to heresy and, during the periodic lulls of intolerance, Lutheranism, at first, then Calvinism, had secured itself an influential though widely dispersed body of adherents. Neither the peasantry nor the city of Paris proved amenable to Calvinistic discipline, but the high provincial nobility and urban middle class in the provinces found it attractive. The struggles, however, broke out within (and not between) classes and within geographical areas. Religion was entangled with political differences between nobles and Crown, and between nobles and nobles. The key to events lay in the impotence of the French monarchy. Francis II, a sickly youth married to Mary Queen of Scots, died in 1560, to be succeeded by a child of ten (Charles IX), who slept in his mother's room. After fourteen years of dependence he was, in turn, succeeded by a brother, Henry III, who spent his evenings at balls, dancing and mincing effeminately, clad in satins of shocking hue. High times induced fits of remorse in him, during which he would flagellate himself and enjoy exquisite pangs of contrition.

As one might expect, the mother of these fops and weaklings, Catherine de Medici (wife of Henry II), was a powerful creature and the dominant political figure of the period. Strong willed she was, and shallow minded she was, but capricious only when her maternal and political interests were at stake. Her twin policies were to exert maximum influence over her children and to escape the overweaning influence of the powerful Guise family. Prodigiously wealthy, and closely related to the royal line by marriage, the Guises were well situated to supervise royalty, especially when it seemed so contemptible.

Guise ambition—ultra Catholic—was counterbalanced by the De Conde family, who were Huguenots, related to the King of Navarre. And other families played their part. France was in turmoil as a result of weak monarchy and religious dissension, and also because the French nobility, as a whole, were entering on a period of profound dislocation.

A century earlier the feudal nobility had been the feudal cavalry —their military function justified their existence. But with the development of the cannon and the rising importance of infantry the nobility lost some of their military preeminence. And, similarly, their traditional functions and importance in local affairs was being transferred slowly but surely to the urban bourgeoisie. This emasculation was aggravated by the growing populousness of the class itself. In England only the firstborn son assumed a title, whereas in France all the children of a noble family were nobles. And this natural increase was compounded by masses of new enoblements, for since titles could be sold, enoblements were a lucrative source of income for the Crown. Inevitably this proliferation of titled and privileged people meant a dimunition of social, political, and military function, and exascerbated pent-up frustrations.

Catherine was essentially secular-minded; she allowed Huguenots freedom of worship throughout the countryside and in the suburbs of the towns—but she underestimated the depth of religious ill feeling on both sides. Retainers of the Duke of Guise slew some Huguenots and immediately Prince de Conde called Protestants to arms without so much as consulting the Crown. As the two armies fought each other to a standstill, Catherine was able to reimpose a pacification slightly less generous than earlier (1563). De Conde, whose concern for Protestantism never interfered with his ambitions for himself, broke the peace with a wildcat scheme to capture the King (1567), a plot so reckless and ill-advised that it brought out the full fury of Catherine's maternal feelings. No quarter was given on either side; butchery was rampant and the mobs joined in the business of hunt and kill with blind relish. Although Catherine was prevailing, the prospect of a financial collapse and the ominous rise of Guise influence caused her to negotiate another peace, still tolerating Protestantism but restricting its practice further than before.

Still the Guises would be satisfied by nothing short of total victory. Capitalizing on Catherine's estrangement from them, a middle group proposed to polish over the religious dissensions by marrying Catherine's daughter to the Protestant Henry of Navarre. The match was concluded, but unfortunately at the same time Catherine began to suspect that the Huguenots were trying to turn her prince from his proper affection to his mother. She rapidly became desperate and prevailed upon Charles to abandon his friends. The Huguenots, she charged, were plotting against his life. The young King's sudden reversal of affection, so grati-

François Dubois, *The Massacre of Saint Bartholomew's Day* (Bibliothèque Publique de Genève).

fying to his mother, doomed the Huguenots to indescribable terror. On St. Bartholomew's Day (August 24, 1572), the tocsin gave the sign for Roman Catholic nobles, led by the Guises, to seek out and slaughter any Huguenots they could lay their hands on. Conde and Navarre, who were in Paris, escaped death only by professing Catholicism. And Paris' blood bath was repeated in the provinces. Needless to say, Protestants everywhere were appalled and aghast, while the Pope and Phillip II of Spain were delighted. The fortress of La Rochelle alone held out for the Huguenots and it became the symbol of resistance. Peace (1573) once more guaranteed liberty of conscience and liberty of worship in La Rochelle and other specified towns.

Still the ultra Catholics could not abide the idea of toleration, and the Huguenots wanted to enlarge the areas in which they were permitted to worship. So under Henry III the tensions never relaxed, though the country might profitably have adopted the mood if not the practice of the court where all was gaiety and relaxation. Henry surrounded himself with what a contemporary called "princes of Sodom" and paid scant attention to anything but his companions.

While Henry played and Catherine aged, the Guises whipped up Catholic feeling to such a pitch that the King was forced to capitulate to them. He revoked every concession that had ever been granted to the Huguenots (1585) and it looked as though St. Bartholomew's Day was come again. A war erupted, known as the War of the Three Henries: Henry III; Henry, Duke of Guise; and Henry of Navarre, the Huguenot. Henry III solved one difficulty by having the Duke of Guise murdered, which raised such a storm of protest against him that he was driven into alliance with Henry of Navarre. Then a zealous friar assassinated him, not realizing, perhaps, that his act left the heretic Henry of Navarre as heir to the throne.

Henry IV was a man of affairs and ability, and of bluff and ready charm. A man's man, he changed the tone at Court noticeably. Religion was not all in all for him, but the loyalty of the Huguenot supporters was never forgotten. He embraced Catholicism only when he was securely on the throne and could guarantee the Huguenots all they had fought for. He negotiated with his foes, buying them off in one case, and defeating them by armed might in others. After concluding a treaty with Spain, he issued the Edict of Nantes (1598), which ensured to Protestants rights of worship in every township where worship had been recently practiced. Huguenot schools and colleges were promised support, and certain fortresses, like La Rochelle, were handed over for a specified period as security for these provisions.

This settlement was virtually a reversion to the situation in 1562, four decades earlier. Had nothing changed? Indeed it had. The depleted ranks of the nobility were filled with new and loyal creations. Yet their growing loss of function was not repaired. After more than a generation of intermittent anarchy, all classes rallied to a strong and centralized Crown. So the cycle of a weak followed by a strong monarchy, centuries old in France, reasserted itself. To be sure, the Crown was impoverished, but all the means were at hand to make up the deficits. One might imagine that past experience would have laid religious hatred and bigotry to rest, but this was not to be. The legacy of the religious wars was not so much mutual forebearance and tolerance as incipient despotism.

# 8

# Old Worlds and New

The religious wars mark the extent of the religious and political disintegration of the past two and a half centuries. Also, the wars illustrate the complexity of the relationships between political and religious ideas. In general, it can be said that Protestantism pitted a Pauline pessimism about man's nature against the Catholics' optimism about human potential. But in the shifting alliances of groups and parties, altruism and intellectual commitment were often less prominent than ambition and momentary expediency. In Calvin's Geneva, for instance, opposition to him came from old established families whose traditional influence was threatened by the energetic Protestants; and doubtless, while they thought Calvin's view of man somewhat peculiar, they found his undermining their former authority quite intolerable. Similarly, in France, those who led the resistance to the Crown found Calvinism congenial to their political aims, yet Prince DeConde prudently declared himself a Catholic when his life stood in danger, and Prince Henry of Navarre thought Paris, and the throne of France, were well worth a Mass. For many, concern for power overrode religious niceties.

Besides such politiques, however, there were others who sacrificed their lives for what they believed to be the good of their souls. Hundreds of Protestants suffered the fires of persecution under Mary Tudor, and a few diehard Puritans were hanged, in turn, by Anglicans in the time of Elizabeth for conscience's sake. Religion for such as these was not a cloak to be donned and doffed at will.

In this maze of motivations there are some tantalizing links between religious affiliations and class affiliations which suggest that some psychic attractions were at work between forms of worship and social needs. One need not be deterministic about it: the spread of religious types depended largely on the accidents of where channels of communication were open or closed. Wherever Protestant ideas could circulate, Calvinism appealed to educated commoners and not, by and large, to members of the nobility, though there were exceptions. Lutheranism found strong aristocratic support and royal backing in Scandinavia and Germany, for Lutheranism appealed to those who favored reform and detested social disruption. Anabaptism, with its millenarian dreams of a heaven on earth, could stir the dispossessed to revolutionary fervor as no other movement could. Within Protestantism it seems that the greater the degree of social deprivation, the higher is the level of enthusiasm needed in worship to make it emotionally satisfying. One scholar has seen "a principle of social compensation" in this process.

There is a clear direction to the spread of Protestantism westward and northward away from the seat of papal authority. This movement corresponds roughly with the shift in commercial leadership to nations on the Atlantic seaboard. Historians have debated interminably about the relationship between Protestantism and capitalism, but that France remained Catholic and Scotland and Scandinavia backward should give pause to any glib and easy theories of a causal connection.

One generalization, however, is worth making about the republican implications of Calvinism as against the autocratic tendencies of Lutheranism and Catholicism. Wherever it spread, Calvinism undermined royal pretensions while Lutheranism and Catholicism both bolstered princely power. Calvinists erected an ecclesiastical structure in which power was shared between clergy and representatives of the congregation. Here was imbedded a revolutionary principle in church affairs: a representative system instead of a monarchy. And, in turn, the Church in which members of the congregation could participate so fully became a school of experience which conditioned members to clamor for a voice in affairs of state. Republicanism in the Church, and in the state, demanded that sovereignty be shared; and republicanism made headway wherever sizeable groups of Calvinists existed. This is not to imply that Calvinists were democrats. Extremer sects who split from the Calvinists often carried the participative and congregational principles to more radical conclusions in both church and state. In contrast to these groups, Calvinists maintained a narrow oligarchy. But, in the context of the 16th century, Calvinism was much feared by conservatives for its radicalism.

Calvin had allowed the right of resistance to constituted authorities only to "inferior magistrates" and a new-found Moses, but these strict limits covered a variety of cases: they could apply to Knox (Moses) and the Scottish lairds and nobles, or to William of Orange and the Netherlands' Estates; to members of the English House of Commons or the French Estates-General. Radical political treaties on sovereignty drew their rationale from scriptures — a covenant existed between governors and governed, and when it was violated by rulers failing to protect their people or failing to observe the "fundamental laws and liberties" of the land, then rulers could and ought to be disobeyed. If Caesar's and God's wills ever clashed a Christian's first duty was to God. Covenant thinking was an early form of the contract theories which became so popular in the 17th and 18th centuries. New images clothed old reasonings: the vague fundamental laws and liberties of the 16th and early 17th centuries became the inalienable rights of later times. Occasionally a Catholic theorist justified the right of rebellion by arguing that a prince became a tyrant when he threatened his subjects' immortal souls, in which case it was no sin to remove him. Theories upholding the divine legitimation of kings were countered by ideas of the ultimate sovereignity of "the people". As a group in the English House of Commons put it, in 1604, "The voice of the people, in things of their knowledge, is said to be as the voice of God." Absolute moral obligations faced other compelling imperatives, and divine rights were set against divine rights. Modern soul-searching about abuses of power and the propriety of civil disobedience has its origin in these religio-political debates.

Generally, Lutheranism and Catholicism stressed the inner rather than the outer aspect of spiritual freedom. Both preached obedience to the secular arm as a binding moral duty, and both survived comfortably in strict monarchical states. In recent times both failed to stand effectively against the rise of dictatorial and totalitarian movements, but since the Second World War, and since the Second Ecumenical Council, there are indications that this tradition of political submissiveness could change.

That a peculiar church form encouraged Calvinists to seek a share in sovereignty does not mean that Calvinists were also advocates of toleration. The discipline of their church was as rigorous as that of the state; the intolerance of the congregation was as constraining as the intolerance of secular authority. Intolerance was never the preserve of any one system; it flourished in monarchy, in oligarchy, and it has been known to flourish in democracy.

Rather than tolerance, Calvinism moulded a distinctive character type, and man with a degree of conscience unknown in other religions. Catholicism provided a conscience-stricken person with the outlet of frequent expiations through penance and sacrament; Lutheranism encouraged the sinner to throw himself on the mercy of Christ to feel the ecstatic inner joy that comes with sublime assurance. Calvinism offered no such rituals for purification; it assumed that guilt was ever present. Mass or Eucharist could never wipe the slate of conscience clean, and conscience sat like the old man of the sea on one's shoulders forever. Calvinists made a fetish of conscience. Yet often the Calvinist was self-righteous and morally callous; his conscience was self-centered rather than socially concerned. This was a conscience with severe drawbacks as well as with merits, a special conscience; but insofar as Calvinists carried it into every sphere of their daily lives as a matter of cosmic duty they illustrate a far wider theme in the history of the later 16th century.

The medieval dichotomy between the sacred and the profane was being replaced by a pervasive and free mingling of theological dogma with all aspects of life. A cosmic seriousness suffuses the art of the later Renaissance: Raphael's *Disputa* was a theological polemic; Dürer sketched vivid sermons on paper; Michelangelo painted a vast religious epic, replete with Biblical allegories, on the roof of the Sistine Chapel. In Spain, the work of El Greco captured the militant spirit of the Jesuits and also embodied the ecstasy of the mystics. El Greco's (1541-1614) hues were dark blacks, greys, and pallid lighter shades; his figures were elongated, their faces wearing a pious and prayerful aspect. *The Burial of the Count of Orgaz* exactly fits the dimension of the wall above the count's tomb and this setting lends an intimate, tactile quality to the spiritual apotheosis painted there. The

El Greco, The Burial of the Count of Orgaz (Anderson, Art Reference Bureau, Church of St. Tome, Toledo).

distinctions between the earthly and the unearthly were being blurred, so the 17th century would inherit two contrary tendencies: one, to remake the earth in conformity with notions of heaven; the other, to review beliefs of heavenly things in the light of earthly knowledge.

This interweaving of worldly and spiritual themes is exemplified by the end to which Margaret of Navarre (1492-1549), sister of Francis I of France, turned the unrestrained, post-Boccaccian tradition of *risqué* short stories. Her *Heptameron* used the old form for uplifting and morally instructive purposes.

A similar trend can be discerned in the serious work of Lope de Vega, possibly Spain's greatest and certainly its most prolific author. He wrote drama, religious and historical epics, as well as pastoral poetry and comedies. Comedy itself became a vehicle for savage and probing social comment. Cervantes' *Don Quixote* can be read as a spiritual physiognomy of Spanish life. Quixote and Sancho Panza represent the polar contrasts within Spain herself, of romance, of chivalry, and of idealism, and also of coarseness, baseness, and rampant cynicism. The Spain of the past is held against the Spain of the present, the foolish and noble against the mundane and crass.

A world was passing, and authors tried bravely to revive it. In Italy, indeed in all Europe, following the pessimism of Machiavelli, Guicciardi, Luther and Calvin, a resplendent literature of chivalry and heroism captured public taste. The courage and the high endeavor of this kind of writing were actually lost possibilities for the Italy of the late 16th century. Returning to epic style for their form, authors were creating a feeling of nostalgia. Ludovico Ariosto (1474-1533) cast back to the days of Charlemagne for a drama of infidelity and its retribution by the Christian Roland against the heathen Saracens in *Orlando Furioso,* or Roland Enraged. The Christian-versus-heathen motif was taken up by Torquato Tasso in *Gerusalemme Liberata,* or Jerusalem Freed, which chronicled that first Crusade when Christians captured Jerusalem. Here, for a moment, the grandeur and nobility of the past were revived to strut in stylized postures of good and evil.

Right triumphed over evil, but peace and victory did not always prevail. In Guarini's (1538-1612) *Il Pastor Fido,* or The

Faithful Shepherd, there is a tone of pessimism and a strain of tragedy in a love comedy. Simplicity and guilelessness were being mixed with darker forces. The "majestical" heavens could be called "a foul and pestilent congregation of vapours," and man, so "noble in reason" and "infinite in faculty," could be seen as "quintessence of dust" (Shakespeare, *Hamlet*, Act II sc. 2). The Frenchman, Montaigne (1533-1592), author of the celebrated *Essays*, passed through a phase of profound skepticism. Unlike Erasmus, whose questionings were shallower, he was driven to probe and test the fundamental tenets of his religious faith. Perhaps nothing better illustrates the mood of doubt infusing Renaissance optimism than Claudio Montiverdi's opera *Orpheo* —the first extant opera performed in musical history in 1607. In glowing phrases, reminiscent of Pico's *Oration on the Dignity of Man*, a chorus vaunts man's powers just before Orpheus fails and Eurydice succumbs to her second death. The opera proceeds with Orpheus' piteous lamentations, lamentations for a world of lost delights.

For the first time for centuries in the history of the west there was an audience receptive to and ready to be moved by tragedy. The exuberance of the past seemed to be hollow, and a sense of doubt and decay seemed to represent the bitter realities of life much more closely than the heady optimism of previous generations. Indeed, the word Faustian that we use to describe the Renaissance's overweening ambition and its superhuman hopes comes from a tragedy, *Dr. Faustus*, by Christopher Marlowe (1564-1593). Faustus cheerfully sold his soul to the devil for unlimited power, pleasure and knowledge. He was not afraid to do so, for he thought hell was a fable, a mere old wives' tale. Ultimately the skeptical and worldly-wise doctor learns the dreadful truth and descends into the cavern of hell. The knowledge that he sought was necromancy, improper knowledge, and after he gained it he used it merely to impress his colleagues and do parlor tricks for potentates. One wonders whether Marlowe was subtly castigating the new knowledge of the Renaissance and the uses to which it was put in his day.

Nowhere were irony and tragedy more forcefully exploited than in England. Even more than Marlowe, William Shakespeare (1564-1616) was the master of the sardonic twist. In *The Mer-*

*chant of Venice,* for example, the Jewish usurer, representing the old law (Jews had long since been banished from England), demands that the letter of the law be levied on his debtor. Portia, the debtor's counselor and lover, pleads for the new law, the Law of the Gospel, but her pleas fall on deaf ears. Shylock will not relent, only to be trapped by the rigidity of the law which he himself advocates: he may have his pound of flesh, no more, no less, else his life is forfeit.

Shakespeare raised tragedy to consummate perfection. As in classical tragedies, his dramas were worked out against a backdrop of cosmic and natural order. Wrongs have been committed against the order of nature and retribution inexorably follows. In *Hamlet* there are murder, adultery, and the consuming passion of revenge. In *Macbeth* the crimes are vaulting ambitions and murder most foul; in *King Lear* the discord is a father's unnatural spurning of a loving daughter; in *Romeo and Juliet* there is civil disorder and a sudden passion; in *Othello* jealousy and a devilish tempter. Terror, pity, passion, and compassion lead to their inevitable climax in death and violent destruction. Within this *métier,* Shakespeare worked with an unrivaled flair for drama: his theatre is enthralling, though one may not believe in witches or ghosts. As Dr. Johnson once observed, there are no heroes in his plays, only men. His characters touch universal chords of experience, they are unbound by time and place, and he clothed his perceptive human insights in the richest language and verse, especially in brilliant free verse. But it is the sense of the cosmos that interests us here, for it must have been shared by his audience.

The cosmos was, above all, a place of settled hierarchical order and harmony. So it had been for centuries. This was the cosmos which the painters of the 1400's had sought to mirror. By the 16th century the reality of flux and change had begun to disturb the harmonies of art and to appear more frequently in vernacular literature. Disturb the cosmos, Shakespeare thought, and ruin would surely follow. In *Troilus and Cressida* Ulysses muses,

> The heavens themselves, the planets, and this centre
> Observe degree, priority, and place,
> Insisture, course, proportion, season, form,

Office, and custom, and in all line of order . . . .
T̩ake but degree away, untune that string,
And hark what discord follows . . .

This serried universe observed change within its prescribed motions. The cycle of seasons, the ebb and flow of the tide, the periods of the moon, the ceaseless changes of day into night, these were of a piece with the repetitive nature of things. Thus the last cantos of Spenser's (1552?-1599) *Fairie Queen,* called the Cantos of Mutabilitie, make mutability an integral part of orderly creation.

The cosmos of the 16th century—the great chain of harmonious being—seems archaic to us now, just as our conceptions will seem silly to future generations. Few of us now believe that stars influence our destinies, or that planetary motions effect our health, though we still use astrological symbols in medicine, for male ( ♂ ) and female ( ♀ ), for example,—a relic of the old connection. A fire and brimstone Hell, white winged angels, and a personified Satan do not wring assent from many in the 20th century. These symbols and allegories represented what were felt to be facts of the human condition. Symbol became fact. Although the symbols of the past have been largely rejected, our moral condition seems no better if perhaps no worse for it. One should not decry Dante for portraying the levels of Hell so literally, but strive to grasp, by taking an imaginative leap, what insights, values and assumptions Dante was expressing within his hieratic structure, through the medium of his highly developed symbolic apparatus.

Few of us now believe in witches, and we give our disoriented and psychotic citizens shock and other milder treatments rather than burn them or hang them or exorcise their devils. Belief in witchcraft, we might think, was a residue of old lore, a relic of residual subterranean paganism from ancient times. It has been pointed out that the early Middle Ages never spawned a witch craze as widespread and as bloodthirsty as the terror of the Renaissance and Reformation. Catholics (especially Dominicans), and Protestants outdid each other in devising tortures and discovering culprits. Ideological conflicts and uncertainty shriveled and hardened the small shell of social tolerance. We, who have witnessed in our time massacres of innocents and known virulent racism, may not be surprised that an "age of light" nursed and suckled psychopathic delusions.

It does surprise us to learn that good health in this period was thought to be the result of a proper balance between the four governing humors of the body. Robert Burton's *The Anatomy of Melancholy* (1621) is a delightful quarry for the sophisticated medical knowledge of the late 16th century. Man lived on food that was assumed to be composed of four basic elements—earth, water, air, and fire—and when the food reached the liver it was there transformed into liquid substances called humors—of melancholy, phlegm, blood and choler—corresponding respectively to the four elements. These fluids sustained the heat and the life of the body. The liver was regarded as the chief lower organ of the body. The heart was king of the middle section of man. By using the heat of the air from the lungs and by refining the blood, the heart was able to replenish all the arteries in the body. The heart governed the middle and the lower portions of man. It was the seat of the passions, and it could mediate between the lower animal sector and the higher rational and immortal portion whose impulses sprang from the brain. The brain, in turn, was divided into three parts, the lower containing the senses, the middle the common sense and the understanding, and the higher part the rational faculty and the soul.

Character was assumed to be formed by the dominance of one humor over another. A phlegmatic man was one in whom phlegm predominated. Sickness, of course, implied a total imbalance of humors or the putrifying or burning of one of them. Medical skill was therefore directed at cooling and quieting disturbed humors and setting them to proper balance again. Diagnosis was usually based on an examination of a patient's urine. Blood-letting (or leeching) was commonplace; emetics and purgatives were frequently prescribed; medical remedies were of the rabbit's-foot variety: the blood of a vulture mixed with two herbs, making a sauce, smeared on lepers, would improve them perceptibly. A good amount of fresh cow dung mixed with wormwood and a small quantity of egg shells crushed could cure a fever. Contagion was thought to be the result of contact with a diseased person or with their clothing, or of proximity to the minute particles of putrifaction which they might exhale. This was not a bad working insight; knowledge of bacteria and viruses did not arrive for centuries and, even today, is largely reserved to the well-educated.

The absence of effective medical knowledge, despite great progress in anatomy, the unhampered course of diseases, the frequency of death, particularly the deaths of women and children in childbirth, the filth and stench of streets—these would comprise the most horrifying aspect of Renaissance life to any modern person unfortunate enough to be transplanted backward in time.

So it is that the lilting love and pastoral lyrics, and the sweet madrigals of the later Renaissance cohabit a world beside the somber awareness of death. Sir Walter Raleigh, a paragon of the romantic adventurer, ended his *History of the World* with this paean:

> O eloquent, just, and mighty Death! whom none could advise, thou hast persuaded; what none hath dared, thou hast done; and whom all the world flattered, thou only hast cast out of the world and despised; thou hast drawn together all the far-stretched greatness, all the pride, cruelty and ambition of man, and covered it over with these two narrow words, *Hic jacet!*

The abiding sense of doubt that we saw in Marlowe and Montaigne, the sense of tragedy, the belief that perhaps the high endeavor of the Renaissance there lay profound futility, the unease, the self-doubt and critical self-transcendence, the stoicism in the face of final things, all these qualities twist and mar the limpid picture of an optimistic Renaissance. While the common assumptions about the cosmos link the Renaissance most closely to the past, the literature of the late 16th century exposes an understanding of change and a capacity to doubt that seem relatively new. Change was not always welcomed; there was a good deal of nostalgia. Change was often equated with decay; there was a sense of loss and longing for a world that was passing, and anxiety about what was to come.

It has been argued that, notwithstanding the medieval survivals and these novel notes of disquiet and foreboding, the humanists of the 15th and 16th centuries prepared the way for the imaginative discovery of new cosmologies by surrounding new discoveries with optimism. By emphasizing the capacities of man, and by boasting, sometimes adolescently, of his prowess, by applauding their own emergence from the thick Gothic night into the glorious sunlight of knowledge and rationality, the humanists created a climate highly favorable to change. It is an ingenious conjecture.

Certainly a critical rationalism of the sort approved by humanists came to infect both Catholic and Protestant orthodoxies in the later 16th century, just as art and literature had been invaded by the renewed spirituality of the Reformation and Counter-Reformation. Heresies like Socianism and Unitarianism, that denied the truth of the doctrine of the Trinity, made headway all over Europe. Arminianism, named after a Dutch theologian, Arminius (1560-1609), shattered the peace of the Dutch and the English churches by decrying as too rigorous the Calvinist doctrine of double predestination. Arminians urged, in humanistic vein, that man had some choice in the matter of his destiny—at least, he could deny his inheritance of grace and damn himself. Eventually such rational and liberal impulses were to turn many an Anglican, Calvinist, and Catholic into a Latitudinarian.

A questing spirit and a lust for new knowledge bolstered all of the intellectual achievements of the period, yet other civilizations had fostered curiosity, so there is nothing particularly distinctive about either the Renaissance or the Reformation on this score. What are distinctive are the fresh styles and fresh solutions found, and the original methods and novel problems discovered in every sphere of activity from religion to science. There is, of course, no special, inherent virtue in these advances. The questions asked by the medieval past were not valueless (indeed, far from it), but doubts had been sown about both questions and answers: superstitions had been scoffed at by humanists and reformers alike, and a long, arduous process of winnowing true belief from superstition had to begin. New questions had to be sown, new answers reaped, and new superstitions concocted to satisfy new needs and slake man's insatiable desire for knowledge.

In science particularly, the pace of inquiry that had long been known and followed in the Middle Ages quickened. Leonardo Da Vinci's notebooks are a jungle of fanciful questionings, some of them misleading and some of them penetrating. Although Leonardo's contributions to science have been grossly overrated by his devotees, he did observe movements of air and water most meticulously, and he did improve various measuring devices. He noticed that air and water moved similarly and discovered some basic principles in hydrodynamics. He was, in many ways, a supremely gifted dilettante. All of his work was unfinished, even his few paintings. This was the net result of seventy years of ceaseless activity.

Leonardo was also one of the first to express nature in mathematical terms. And this mathematical personification, this symbolic and abstract representation of reality, is now recognized as one of the bases of modern science. Mathematics was beginning to have some success in solving concrete physical problems like the movement of projectiles, which had been posed by the appearance of cannon in warfare. A host of natural philosophers in the 16th century spent their lives and talents solving cubic and even more exotic equations and improving on the available algebraic symbolism, making steps toward the analytic geometry that Descartes was able to use and develop extensively.

Above all, Copernicus opened the way for a full mathematical development of astronomy by reconstructing a universe in which the earth both revolved on its axis and revolved around the sun. His conclusion was based quite as much on imagination as on observation; he realized that some rethinking was necessary after finding contradictions between earlier authorities. Some of these calculated the motions of the spheres on the basis of concentric circles; others used eccentric spheres; and still others used epicycles. He tried to bring a simple and acceptable uniformity to these contradictions. He was much influenced by the neoplatonic preference for the sun as the center of things; and his theory was open to grave objections on this and other grounds. The beginnings of astronomy, then, were surrounded with a good deal of misinformation and error.

Tycho Brahe was the first to realize that the postulates of the Copernican system had to be tested by careful observation. The appearance of what was, to the world, a new star (actually it was a dying star) in 1572 caused Tycho to suggest, timidly, the mutability of the celestial substance; and a comet of 1577 seemed, with the superior instruments he had developed, to have passed beyond the sun through what had been thought to be the solid celestial spheres to which the planets were presumably affixed. Indeed, the orbit of this comet seemed to have been oval rather than circular. Tycho left his masses of data to his pupil, Kepler (1550-1631).

Kepler worked out the orbit of Mars according to the Ptolemaic, the Copernican, and the Tychonic systems, and the discrepancies between the results led him to formulate two laws: (1) planets move in elipses, with the sun in one focus; (2) planets do not move at uniform speed, but at varying speeds, so that a line joining the planet's center to the sun would sweep out an equal area in an equal time. That a planet's speed varied with its distance from the sun aroused intense interest in the phenomenon of attraction. Magnetism, just beginning to be studied, became a dominating concern in the next century. Kepler had broken the "spell of circularity," and he had managed to smash the myth of a simple harmony in the cosmos, without discarding the idea that the complex harmonies of the universe could yet be reduced to simple laws. His two laws were contained in writings published in 1609; his third did not appear for another decade.

Much of his work depended on improvements made on Greek geometry by the mathematicians of the 16th century. He depended, too, on improved methods in computation, like the use of decimal fractions, and on the discovery of logarithms by a Scot, John Napier, in 1614. Elaborate tables for trigonometrical use were now available for astronomers.

But, ultimately, Kepler's discoveries arose from his search for the underlying harmonies that lay behind physical reality and from his desire to express those harmonies in numerical relations. These numerical relations represented, for him, the true nature of things. Thus, Kepler's inquiries were metaphysical in scope rather than strictly scientific. His discoveries appear alongside and are imbedded in discussions on the nature of the Trinity, of the Source of Celestial Harmony, and so on. Kepler believed, along with the neoplatonic philosophers and artists, that archetypal ideas existed in God's mind from eternity, and that

God reproduced these both in the universe and in the human mind. His search for observable laws in nature was a search for just such a portion of God's mind as He wished to reveal to man, and the visible universe was a sign of a greater intangible Reality.

So, in the Renaissance, science was not yet the secular and functional business that we imagine it is today. It developed within the broad confines of metaphysics that seem outlandish and strange. The religious and the scientific were still fused; the one encouraged the other; but at the same time, science was extending and corroding religious cosmologies. One thing was clear from the work of the astronomers: the closed world had become an infinite universe. In the centuries to follow, man's place in this universe, and God's, would need to be defined and defined again to give man the wise sentiment he seems to crave in the face of bewildering reality.

# Index